A HISTORY OF SEAFARING – VOLUME II

THE DISCOVERERS

Telonium

Mōnzquita

Fanū Indorum

The Discoverers

BY RICHARD ARMSTRONG

FREDERICK A. PRAEGER, *Publishers*

New York · Washington

BOOKS THAT MATTER

Published in the United States of America in 1969
by Frederick A. Praeger, Inc., Publishers
111 Fourth Avenue, New York, N.Y. 10003

© 1968, in England, by Richard Armstrong

Maps and drawings by Ivan Lapper

Library of Congress Catalog Card Number: 68-54001

Printed in Great Britain

Contents

Maps

Build-up to Break-through

1 PTOLEMY'S WORLD

THE PRIMARY CONCERN of the seafarer has always been transport, the carrying of people and goods – especially goods – from port to port about the world. In a way he invented commerce and he has existed for and by it ever since. Nevertheless and incidentally he has been other things besides a carrier. From time to time he figures in the histories as a fighting man (usually reluctant if not actually press-ganged), a pirate, a buccaneer, a slaver, a trader, a missionary, even as an empire-builder and administrator of a kind. But leaving aside the long-term effect of his shuttling to and fro on the exchange of ideas and their development, possibly his biggest and certainly his most dramatic contribution to human progress was made as a discoverer.

He functioned thus in a big way from the middle of the 15th till the end of the 18th centuries, though some authorities make the truly significant period shorter than that. One indeed (A. P. Newton in *The Great Age of Discovery*) narrows it down to the span of a single lifetime, reckoning it began in 1477 and ended in 1527. He sees this half-century as the crucial period of the great surge forward by mankind that has become known as the Renaissance and declares:

> . . . The one central and unprecedented fact of the time which never can be repeated or even paralleled in any future age was the sudden expansion of the habitable world by geographical discovery. . . .   [p 4]

If that refers to anything it is to the seafarer's part, and it is fair enough; but it is an academic reading and the golden age of the flesh and blood mariner undoubtedly lasted over the next three hundred odd years as well.

It was in this period that he demonstrated most fully the qualities of resourcefulness, daring, cold courage, tenacity of purpose and endurance that mark him out as different; and it was in this period that he reached the peak of public esteem, achieved his greatest social prestige and received the highest honours in the gift of land-bound mortals.

Discovery, of course, was always an inescapable by-product of his normal activity. He had opened up the Mediterranean basin and found a way by sea to northern Europe long before the Christian era began; and all through the Dark Ages, he was pushing his luck north and westward from Scandinavia; but until the middle of the 15th century he was hedged in by apparently insoluble problems and his world was still that of the Ancients. He knew more about it than the early geographers, having travelled it more extensively; but his overall picture, the boundaries both his experience and his imagination gave to it, were essentially the same as Ptolemy's and often very much less precise. And Ptolemy, let it be noted, lived in the first half of the second century AD.

7

This Claudius Ptolemaeus, to give him his full name, was centuries ahead of his time and is numbered among the world's great men. He was born in Egypt and worked in Alexandria when that famous city was the centre of learning for all the known world. As a mathematician he developed the practical applications of trigonometry; he also wrote on music and on optics; but above all else he was an astronomer and geographer. His summary of Greek astronomy, the *Syntaxis*, was accepted as the last word on the subject until 1543 when Copernicus blew it all sky-high by demonstrating the revolutionary theory that the sun is the centre of our planetary system and we revolve round it instead of it round us.

Ptolemy's other great work was the *Geographia* and this remained the basic authority on the physical characteristics of the world until the Renaissance. The book, like many others, was lost in the shadows of the Dark Ages, but it came to light again in 1406 when it was translated into Latin and immediately set forward-looking, fearless men questing along new lines of thought.

At a time when science was inextricably mixed up with mysticism and magic, Ptolemy came nearer to a true scientific approach than anybody else did for centuries. The philosophers of his day and before him produced many basically sound ideas and theories. They proposed very early on, for instance, that the world was a sphere and earlier still had known that the position of a given place upon its surface – what we now call its latitude – could be determined by observing the altitude of the Pole Star. But instead of going on from there the interpreters of established facts added confusion to obscurity by fitting them willy-nilly into the accepted mystical or religious scheme of things belonging to their time. Ptolemy showed men how to reject authority based on mystical revelation and build only on direct observation.

Ptolemy's work includes maps and tables giving the positions of all the then known cities, seaports, islands and navigable river mouths in the world and the fact that these are never accurate is immaterial. It is the principles he laid down and followed, the methods he devised, that make him great, and his rediscovery was a potent factor in the opening of man's mind and the freeing of his imagination.

So Ptolemy's world was a sphere, a proposition first put forward by Pythagoras around 500 BC, argued beyond refuting by Aristotle a couple of centuries later, and widely accepted by scholars at the beginning of the Christian era. Following the collapse of the *Pax Romana*, however, when the Greek and Alexandrian philosophers sank into obscurity, the Church fought bitterly against the round-earth concept. But its position was impossible to maintain even in an age of darkness and ignorance and by the eighth century official opposition to the idea was withdrawn. After that there were still many people who believed the earth was flat, but generally speaking scholars knew better; and so did the seafarer with his home-port for ever dropping below the sea-rim astern and his landfalls lifting magically out of it ahead. It is doubtful if he ever questioned the spherical shape of the earth and we know for sure that the Arabs – possibly the greatest mariners of ancient times apart from the Phoenicians – were making maps of the world in the shape of silver and bronze globes by the 12th century and likely enough long before. Consequently the rediscovery of the Greek texts of Ptolemy and their translation into Latin came as a challenge to men rather than as the opening up of a store of garnered knowledge.

The fact is that Ptolemy's world was very much misconceived. It consisted of the three known continents – Europe, Africa and Asia – plus a great south land, still

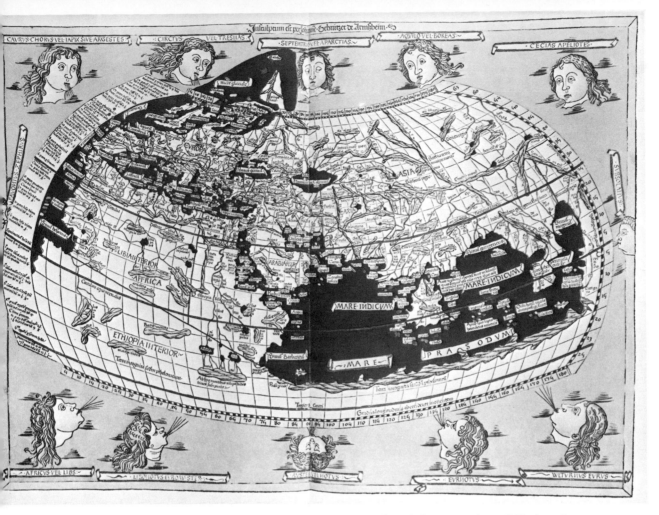

1　Ptolemy's World. Map reproduced from reprint of Ptolemy's
work published at Ulm in 1482. Prepared by N. Germanus.
Note the twelve personified winds – Argestes, Boreas,
Apeliotes, etc.

undiscovered. Most of the Greek philosophers had dreamed up a lost continent somewhere. Plato for instance called it Atlantis and located it far out beyond the Pillars of
Hercules. Ptolemy put it to the south-east of Asia and drew it spreading westward to
join on to Africa thus totally enclosing the Indian Ocean and providing a huge land-
mass below the Equator to balance that above it. The Mediterranean basin had been
travelled and proved; so had the Red Sea and the Indian Ocean north of the Line.
Ptolemy filled in the rest as best he could and throughout the Dark Ages monastic
scholars elaborated to evolve a picture of the world stuffed with concepts that to us
seem utterly ludicrous but were sincerely believed in their day.

Thus man came through the Middle Ages with the firm conviction that the earth
consisted roughly speaking of three parts land and one part water. The liquid element
formed a single vast ocean round which the land-mass was disposed in a never-ending
shore to contain it. Asia began at Jerusalem and extended eastwards for half the
circumference of the globe. Beyond it was the Garden of Eden.

9

2   Marco Polo at Ormuz in the Persian Gulf. From *Livre de Merveilles* with pictures by the Master of The Hours of the Maréchal de Boucicaut

Within this hemisphere Ptolemy's map showed the Nile Valley and the Red Sea, both known in his day as well as the back of a man's hand, the two Arabias – Felix and Deserta – the Persian Sinus (or Gulf), the River Indus and the Indian sub-continent. As exact knowledge diminished imagination took over and beyond Arabia the shape of the land-mass looks to our eyes curiously distorted. Nevertheless the basic elements are there like the bone-structure in a man misshapen with obesity and we can pick out familiar pieces like the Ganges, the Bay of Bengal – here called the Great Sinus – and the long line of South-East Asia down to a fanciful point called Cape Catigara. Among the things beyond our ken are the Island of Taprobana (unless it is Ceylon) and the Kingdom of Prester John.

Excluding the Earthly Paradise part of it, this concept was in general explored overland by Marco Polo, a Venetian who started eastward in 1271 and passing through, among other places, Bagdad, Khorrassan, the Pamirs and Yarkand, crossed the Gobi Desert to reach China and the court of the Great Khan in 1275. He entered the service of the Khan and for several years travelled as his envoy visiting places as far off as Burma, Cochin China and India. His last post was the governorship of Yangchow. This he held for three years then headed west again. He made his return journey via Sumatra, India and Persia and arrived back in Venice in 1295.

In the end, although he had travelled so extensively and was obviously a man of intelligence with a questing, eager mind, Marco Polo did little or nothing to correct or even challenge the common geographical errors of his day. He proved that India could be reached from China by sea and made invaluable commercial contacts connected with the spice trade, but in the main his revelations and discoveries were easily squeezed into the framework of current ideas and even used to confirm them. Consequently Ptolemy's world continued to dominate the thinking of cosmographers for another two centuries.

Among the zany beliefs widely held was that southward from the African shore of the Mediterranean and the Pillars of Hercules lay a zone where the sun was hot enough to burn a man black or shrivel him up into a piece of crackling. In this region it was believed the sea evaporated so quickly in the incredible heat that it became a semi-solid, sticky-like treacle, and ships could make no headway through it even if the crews could survive long enough to get there. Unknown Africa and Asia and even the remoter parts of Europe were supposed to be peopled by strange creatures – men whose heads grew beneath their shoulders; others with a single foot big enough to use as a sunshade, others again with their feet turned backward as a protective device leaving tracks which sent their enemies seeking them in the wrong direction. These monsters were believed to be man-eaters and were credited with other habits and customs too filthy or scarifying to mention.

Such hair-raising, blood-chilling stories probably owed their origin to poverty-stricken seafaring men talking for bed, board and a stoup of wine in quayside taverns; but they became part of the repertory of the countless troubadours, mummers and other kinds of vagabonds wandering over Europe. These were the press-men, the news-mongers of their time, and like all their breed before and since, sensation was more important to them than strict veracity. The scholars and maybe educated people in general were not deceived but these categories fooled themselves in other ways and much more disastrously.

In no way were the pre-Renaissance scholars further out than in their estimates of what we now call longitude. Taking Lisbon as the westernmost city of note in Europe and Shanghai as the easternmost one in China, the distance between is roughly 135 degrees. Ptolemy reckoned it was 210 degrees, while Toscanelli (1397–1482), the Florentine cosmographer who came nearer than any of his contemporaries to getting the length of a degree at the Equator right, was even further out. He made it 256 degrees and added considerably to the subsequent confusion. This enormous exaggeration of the extent of the land-mass eastward led to an equivalent underestimate of the distance to 'the end of Asia' going westward and the ultimate effect was that a third of the earth's surface got lost in the figuring.

Nevertheless Toscanelli was brilliant. Like the Greeks and the Arabs he based himself on research and inquiry and would have nothing to do with mysticism. His contribution to the sum of our knowledge of the equinoxes and other movements of the earth and sun in relation to each other was considerable and in addition he was an enthusiastic map-maker. Some writers call him the greatest cosmographer of his day and undoubtedly his map of 1474, though distorted with misconceptions, is a brave attempt to break free of Ptolemy's thinking and open up new ideas.

The advanced thinking demonstrated in Toscanelli's map was taken up by the German cosmographer, Martin Behaim (1459–1506); but he too was loath to abandon the Ancients and in 1492 he constructed a globe which he himself claimed was based on Ptolemy, Pliny, Strabo and Marco Polo. Behaim was a practical navigator and had voyaged along the West African coast as far as the mouth of the Congo. He bequeathed his globe to his native city of Nuremberg and over a long period enjoyed a very high reputation; but some debunking has been done on him in modern times and he, like his work, is now considerably devalued.

Cosmography and map-making were fashionable pursuits in those days. Followed diligently and with imagination the art could be turned into a lucrative profession with the chance of great wealth and power always just round the corner. So Toscanelli and Behaim were only two among many speculating on the size, shape and nature of the areas of land and sea that make up the earth's surface. In a sense they were dreamers but they were haunted by quite positive questions which prevented them taking off entirely. Africa – was there an end to it somewhere south of the Equator or did it join up with another land-mass enclosing the Indian sea? Asia – where did it really finish? The southern continent, lost Atlantis – did it really exist? Such were the big problems and getting at them involved a host of smaller ones. What made the sea salt? Did it really thicken as it evaporated? And so on.

2 THE PREREQUISITES

However, it was not the muddled thinking of the cosmographers alone that kept man in Ptolemy's world. To get out of it he needed a number of things. First and most important, he needed a suitable ship – one that was easily handled in all weathers, capable of beating to windward and big enough to carry the large quantity of stores, provisions and water needed to maintain the crew in reasonable health and working condition over immensely protracted passages.

Next he needed navigation instruments with which to fix the position of his discoveries and charts on which to record them and mark out the courses made between them.

Given the right ship, instruments and charts, he would still need the money to pay for them and more money again wherewith to buy stores for the voyage and induce men to sail with him, to forsake the soft ways of the land for the hard-lying ones of the sea, to give up the easy, if penurious, security they were enjoying to chase the will-o'-the-wisp of another man's dream with a nebulous prospect of fortune at the end of it and less than a fifty-fifty chance of survival.

Money in those days meant patronage. Short of piracy or large-scale larceny there was no other way of getting it. And patronage was a function of power. It was vested in kings, princes and prelates and dispensed by those who had the ear of them. But for all the idealism of the Crusades and the romantic clap-trap of knights in shining armour, altruism was still a very weak card in anybody's hand. Everyone from the scullion all the way up to the man on the throne had his eye on the main chance and had to be shown what was in it for him before he would stake a groat. This meant that the dream in itself, however rosy, wasn't enough to attract the interest of great men. There had to be something else, something quite apart, acting as a dynamic on him, driving him to back the dreamer as a means to another end.

These indispensable prerequisites for a break-through were slow in coming. Ship design had advanced very slowly if at all through the Dark Ages and though the

Crusades had provided a powerful stimulus the ship-builder had been concerned under it to increase the capacity and stability of his craft rather than to develop those qualities needed by the discoverer. Consequently (as the Andersons point out in their book *The Sailing Ship*) 'at the beginning of the 15th century the big sea-going sailing ship had one mast and one sail. . . . '(p 116). Such a ship was slow even before the wind and liable to capsize or carry her mast away if she got beam on to it; and such a sail was murder for the men who had to handle it. It was altogether too big, too heavy and too clumsy, especially for crews whose strength and vitality had been sapped by scurvy.

This disease was the scourge of the seafarer both before the Renaissance and for a long time after it. Always associated with long passages, it was caused mainly by the absence of fresh meat and vegetables in the diet, though overcrowding, living in cold, damp quarters, prolonged fatigue under unpleasant circumstances and mental depression itself were known to be contributory factors. It was what we now call a deficiency disease, the element lacking being vitamin C. The symptoms could be terrifying, beginning with loss of weight, progressive weakness and anaemia. Then quite quickly the gums would become swollen and spongy and ooze blood at the slightest touch. This loosened the teeth which then began to fall out. After that if the disease was allowed to develop unchecked, spots and blue blotches like bruises would appear first on the legs, then on the arms and the body. Finally the joints would become swollen and stiff and as the action of the heart weakened the body temperature would drop until death came to end the suffering.

Scurvy was a great inhibitor of dreams and the fear of it a powerful anchor for a seafaring man in his home-port. The odds on a seaman falling victim to it increased rapidly with the length of the passage and could easily rise as high as three to one. Men prepared to take that kind of risk are always hard to come by and getting a crew for a voyage of uncertain duration to an unknown destination was another of the discoverer's problems.

As to navigating instruments, there had been progress in this field but here again it was very slow, and the basic problems remained unsolved. Latitude was fairly well understood and for a long time there had been several methods of determining it with great accuracy on land, or even on a ship lying at anchor and absolutely still in a harbour or river mouth; but at sea or lying in an open roadstead where there was even a slight swell it became an uncertain business. Nevertheless, the errors could be largely cancelled out by taking several observations and averaging the result; but the question that really plagued the would-be discoverer and held him back was how to determine his longitude, the distance he had travelled east or west from a given point.

Here again the mathematicians and the astronomers had come up with the right ideas. They knew that the key to it all lay in changing distance into time, that the length a man must travel to get, say, from Cadiz to Catania could be worked out precisely by observing a conjunction of the same two celestial bodies in both places then comparing notes. The phenomenon would occur at a different time in each place and the distance between them, east or west, could be calculated from that difference. The practical problem was how to get the exact time, and the two great needs of the navigator remained a universally recognised prime meridian from which to start counting and a clock that would keep perfect time for extremely long periods under widely varying conditions of climate and movement.

Of course he already had his quadrant or an astrolabe, a compass now too, with

13

portolani to give him courses and distances and even Crusaders' charts on which to plot them and lay off his bearings. Using an hour-glass for the time, he could estimate his speed through the water and from that work out his easting or westing; but the accuracy of a position arrived at in this way depended to some extent on the navigator's experience and a very great deal on his flair for the exercise and instinct for the sea. This was well enough on familiar passages between known places; but nobody was eager to push off into the unknown with nothing more than a dreamer's hunch and a seaman's instinct to guide him.

3 THE DYNAMIC

Of all the conditions required to set up and make possible a break-through in the end it was the dynamic, the overwhelming urge that came first and it sprang out of the need to reconstruct the pattern of world trade shattered by the failure of the Crusades.

That pattern had been slowly built up through the Middle Ages and by the beginning of the 14th century it was completely dominated by the Italian city-states such as Venice, Genoa and Florence. They were the middlemen and the carriers. All the silks, jewels, spices and other luxuries of the Orient flowed into western Europe through them and in their bottoms, and gradually Venice worked herself into the position of chief broker. Newton tells us that in the year 1317 she established a regular service of galleys between the Adriatic and northern Europe and:

> ... By means of these galleys the ginger of Malabar and the cloves of Ternate, the cinnamon of Ceylon and the nutmegs of Malacca, the camphor of Borneo and the aloes of Socotra, not to mention the chinaware from China found their way into English homes.
> ...
> [p 129]

She had factories and depots in all the main ports of the eastern Mediterranean and was firmly and powerfully established at Alexandria and also at La Tana where the River Don flows into the Sea of Azof. These two points were the termini of the caravan routes from the East. It was through Alexandria that she received the cargoes of gems and precious stones from India and of drugs and spices from the Moluccas at the end of a voyage begun in native craft to Calicut, continued from there in Moorish vessels as far as the Red Sea, then carried overland on camels to the Nile and finally dropped down that river to its mouth in dhows. At La Tana she linked up with the caravan routes from China through Turkestan.

Early in the 15th century Jiddeh, the port of Mecca, became the Red Sea terminus and Varthema who visited the place in 1503 wrote that he found there:

> ... a marveylous number of straungers and pylgryms, of the whiche some came from Syria, some from Persia and others from both the East Indies, that is to say, both India within the ryver of Ganges and also the other India without the same ryver [modern Siam and China] I never sawe in anye place, greater abundance and frequentation of people. From India the Greater they have pearles, precious stones and plentie of spyces and especially from Bangalla, they have a very large quantity of cotton and silks. . . . In the lower part of the Temple were fyve or six thousande men that sell none other thyng than sweete oyntmentes and from hence all manner of sweet savours are carried into the countreyes of all the Mohumetans. . . .
> [Hakluyt, d.]

14

3   The Capture of Constantinople by the Turks in 1453. By Tintoretto

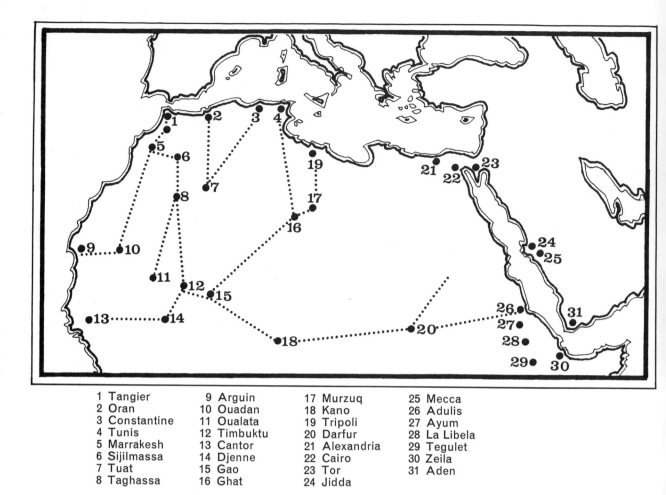

1 Tangier	9 Arguin	17 Murzuq	25 Mecca
2 Oran	10 Ouadan	18 Kano	26 Adulis
3 Constantine	11 Oualata	19 Tripoli	27 Ayum
4 Tunis	12 Timbuktu	20 Darfur	28 La Libela
5 Marrakesh	13 Cantor	21 Alexandria	29 Tegulet
6 Sijilmassa	14 Djenne	22 Cairo	30 Zeila
7 Tuat	15 Gao	23 Tor	31 Aden
8 Taghassa	16 Ghat	24 Jidda	

4   The old trade routes across the Sahara from the Red Sea.
The Arab conquest of the Mediterranean made it impossible
for the spices of the East to be carried by land to north-east
Europe. This was one of the main reasons why a sea route
to India round southern Africa had to be found

It is impossible now to calculate or even hazard a guess as to what this traffic
added up to in terms of wealth and consequent power; but it would be immense by any
standard, even fabulous; and the splendour of Venice today, faded and decaying
though it is, bears witness to it, as do the proud and haughty faces looking out from the
portraits of the Doges.

But all through the later half of the 14th century and the early decades of the
15th, the Moslems were tightening their grip on the trade routes to the East and
imposing ever heavier tolls on the traffic passing along them. The climax came in 1453
when the impossible, the unthinkable, happened and Constantinople, the last Christian
bastion, fell to them. This completed the Arab conquest of the eastern Mediterranean
and the Moslems, proselytising, triumphantly aggressive, finally took over the trade

to the Orient. They refused to allow Christendom any direct contact with Asia and almost overnight the complex system of marketing, so carefully and slowly built up over the centuries, was in ruins.

To the people of that day and particularly to the seafaring and trading elements among them this must have looked like the biggest disaster of all time. Venice and Genoa, Pisa and Florence, countered the blow by building bigger fleets; but it was impossible to break the monopoly of Islam and in the end the city-states turned on each other and fought desperately for what was left of trade and influence in the Mediterranean basin.

Long before this culmination, however, thinking and far-seeing men had read the signs. They knew the Wars of the Cross were doomed to failure and were already facing up to the problems that would follow their final collapse, particularly in Spain and Portugal. Here, as elsewhere in Europe, the Crusades had been a focal point and outlet for other things besides religious fervour: the still hardly suppressed barbarism of the Dark Ages, for instance, military ambition, lust for power, greed for wealth as well as the ordinary man's quite innocent desire to get on and carve out a niche for himself or find a place in the sun. And now all these desires, urges and drives would be adrift and seeking a new road to fulfilment. Until one was found for them they would be both explosive and unpredictable.

That was one headache for the ruling princes and the prelates; the other was the slow but inevitable drying up of their principal sources of wealth. They had learned to live extravagantly and knew no other way; they had surrounded themselves with magnificent trappings and fabulous possessions; they maintained enormous retinues of servants who had to be fed and courtiers who had to be sweetened; and all this had been paid for out of their share in the proceeds of the trade with the East. What were they going to use for money when that trade failed, as fail it must?

The need to break the hardening monopoly of the eastern trade enjoyed by the Arabs, to locate and exploit new sources of wealth and to provide a safe outlet for all the dangerous, driving energy and ambitions frustrated by the pending collapse of the Crusades – here then was the dynamic in the Iberian Peninsula. And there in the Mediterranean basin at Genoa and Venice, Florence and Pisa, were the dreamers, penniless men with ideas seeking for patrons – mathematicians, cosmographers and pilots. And as it always will when the time is ripe, history now threw up a man with both the wit and the urge to gather them together and set them moving.

He was Henry, the fourth son of King John I of Portugal and his wife Philippa who was a daughter of John of Gaunt. Henry was born in 1394 and although he was never a seafaring man, he has become known as Henry the Navigator. J. Holland Rose in his *Man and the Sea* calls him the last of the Crusaders and with some truth for in 1415 he had a final desperate fling against the Moors at Ceuta, a port on the African coast opposite Gibraltar. He was successful too; but war, even the holy kind, was not his line, and though he showed great courage and military prowess in this battle, he had no heart or appetite for fighting. Passionately religious and fanatically Christian, he thought there were other ways of strengthening the hand of God against the heathen. In common with many of his contemporaries he believed the Prester John legend, that somewhere to the east and south of the Nile Valley there was a great and powerful Christian kingdom ruled by a man of that name; and the idea that took hold of him and came to dominate his life absolutely was to find a way by sea round Africa and, by thus out-flanking the Arabs, make contact and join forces with this mighty prince among men.

Abandoning his military career, Henry went to the little port of Sagres, tucked in under the cliffs where Cape St Vincent fronts the Atlantic Ocean. He was a patient man and a splendid organiser, and young enough to start with the fundamentals and make sure of each step before he took the next. His first concern was to set up at Sagres a unique institution that can only be called an academy of the sea; his second to make it the Mecca, a place of pilgrimage for every footloose astronomer, mathematician, cosmographer, chart-maker, ship-designer and pilot in Europe. They came in to him from as far north as the shores of the Baltic and as far east as the Aegean and the coast of Palestine; and in their wake trailed the seafarers, those men of all nations cursed with the itching foot and a taste for living dangerously.

The time was ripe, the need was urgent and the break-through was imminent.

5 Henry the Navigator. By Nuno Gonçalves,
a detail from his famous Triptych of the Infante

To Cathay by the Cape

1 HENRY THE NAVIGATOR (1394–1460)

OF ALL THE GREAT FIGURES produced by the 15th and 16th centuries – and that includes among others Christopher Columbus, Amerigo Vespucci, the Cabots, Magellan and Sir Francis Drake – none matched the first of them all for brilliance, organising ability, inspiring leadership, tenacity of purpose and single-minded devotion. He was that Prince Henry of Portugal known as *the Navigator* and described by one authority as 'the father of continuous maritime discovery'. Yet, though he had so much to do with the foundation of modern geography and indeed with preparing the ground for the enormous stride forward in human knowledge and understanding now known as the Renaissance, Henry belonged absolutely and irrevocably to the Middle Ages. His approach to problems was uncompromisingly scientific and practical; he never fooled himself or tried to fool others by blurring the sharp edges of anything with wishful thinking; but he was always the romantic, the knight of the Cross, the Crusader; and just as his first recorded appearance is in battle against the Moslems at Ceuta, so was his last one against the same foe at Alcazar in 1460. His love-affair with the sea filled all the forty-odd years between.

Newton sums him up as well as anybody who ever wrote about him:

> The sequel we know; one man by faith and persistency, drove a nation to look for its prosperity overseas and launched it on a career of discovery and conquest which in the 16th century took the flag, the Cross of Christ, into every ocean. . . . But the aggrandisement of Portugal was not the main purpose of the Navigator though his countrymen doubtless thought first of their personal interests, nor was it merely the increase of knowledge and still less pecuniary gain which governed his life and acts. Both by inclination and by duty as Governor of the Order of Christ he was first a crusader and sought to stem the advance of Islam . . . he lived like a monk and died a virgin.   [p 46]

From the very beginning Henry knew what he was after and exactly how to go about getting it. The first essential was a suitable ship. As already noted she had to incorporate a number of apparently mutually exclusive opposites in her design. First she had to be big enough to cope with the highest, wildest seas imaginable, capable of maintaining herself and a considerable crew for anything up to two years and at the same time small enough to be easily handled by that same crew weakened by illness or reduced by death. She would need to carry enough sail to drive her at a reasonable speed when the wind was fair and it would have to be so disposed that she could keep going to some extent even when it was foul. Her hull would have to be deep and her lines fine to give her speed and manœuvrability, and at the same time capacious, and with all that, still shallow enough to operate safely among unknown shoals and reefs.

Whether it was blind luck or sound judgment is anybody's guess, but he found his

6 Portuguese Carracks. A painting in oils by Cornelis Anthoniszoon.
The ships belong to the first half of the 16th century and are
described as the type used in the Carreira da India

prototype operating right there under his nose out of Sagres. It was a purely local form
of the lateen-rigged craft common all over the Mediterranean basin and the Portuguese
called it the *caravel*. The Andersons describe her as:

> . . . a fairly small vessel with three lateen sails, the biggest forward and the smallest aft.
> Apparently its stern above the waterline was finished off square instead of having the side-
> planking brought round in the ordinary way. . . .   [p 124]

The words *caravel*, *carrack* and *carvel* are all current around this period and there is some
confusion between them. The Andersons, however, quite definitely identify them as
different types of ship. The *carrack* was the oldest, dating back as far as the 13th century.
It was most closely associated with Genoa and Venice and developed during the 15th
century into the three-master which became the full-rigged ship and remained 'the
same in essentials for about 400 years' (p 120). The *carvel* appears to have been a square-
sterned, flush-planked vessel of the 15th and 16th centuries. The Andersons cite two
examples both famous in their day. One was the *Peter* of La Rochelle, *c.* 1462, and the
other the *Elefant* built in 1532. This last one was a Swedish man-of-war. She was 174
feet long and 40 feet wide and known as 'the great carvel'.

The caravel as Henry found her had a hull-form well adapted for work on an
exposed coast where high seas and heavy swells were the rule rather than the exception.
She had both the kind of lift and the basic stability needed to cope with these conditions
and the complex tide patterns of the area. If need be she was light enough and fine

20

enough in her lines to be rowed against head-winds and adverse currents. Of course as she stood she was totally unsuitable for prolonged deep-water passages and Henry, backed by the best designing brains and the most skilful shipwrights he could muster, set about improving her. How many ideas he tried out and rejected nobody knows but in the end he evolved a craft capable of keeping the high seas indefinitely and still workable by oars. She remained lateen-rigged on main and mizzen but there were square sails on her foremast now and the pictures of her remind one irresistibly of the modern barquentine.

The principle involved in Henry's modification of the sail plan was simple but enormously important. Instead of one single huge sail to a mast, a monstrosity that strained rigging and spar to the limit and broke the hearts of a crew, he spread the same or even a greater effective area of canvas by breaking it up into what are now called *courses* and *topsails*. These were easier to handle and could be more effectively trimmed to the wind. Eventually they evolved into the towering pyramids of sails seen in the *clippers* of the 19th century.

The historians disagree among themselves in detail about the size and rig of Henry's caravel; but this could be taken as proof that her design did not appear overnight but was slowly and continuously evolving through all the forty years of his work at Sagres. Newton describes the craft as:

> . . . little two-masted, half-decked boats of less than 50 tons burden, carrying lateen sails and dependent on wind and tide; their crews did not generally exceed 30 men. . . . [p 45]

F. J. Pohl gives them much bigger dimensions. He says some of them were as long as 100 feet with 25 feet across the beam and 'a capacity of hundreds of tons'. They were faster than Spanish ships and able to sail closer to the wind. It is true Pohl was writing about the two or three decades after the Navigator's death but as the Andersons point out nothing changed so wonderfully slowly as the overall dimensions of ships. The French built one in 1419 at Bayonne that was 186 feet long from stem to sternpost and in 1790 the biggest ship in the world, another Frenchman called *Commerce de Marseille*, was only 211 feet. If they could only make 25 feet in 370 hard-driving competitive years it is not unreasonable to suggest they didn't change at all in the half century covering the great years of discovery.

So having got his ships, Henry's next problem was to find crews for them; and here again he was lucky or maybe just that little bit more perceptive than other organisers. The men he needed, like the prototype of his ship, were there in Sagres.

The Portuguese seamen enjoyed a high reputation in the harbours of the world. They were known to be fearless and enterprising. Seafaring to them was neither a soft option nor a way of life to be followed merely for the gamble. It was a trade, hard and rough, dirty and dangerous but promising rewards adequate to the risk and suffering involved. This approach was just what Henry needed but he knew that by itself it was not enough; he knew there were other hazards than merely getting the feet permanently wet or disappearing for ever into the blue. Seafaring is essentially undramatic; even things like storm and shipwreck have a build-up and seldom, if ever, come on a ship unaware. The rest is routine – the endless repetition of the same simple diurnal pattern. Prolonged indefinitely it becomes death to the human spirit, for the one thing a man needs above all else is a known goal and steady recognisable progress towards it. Without either one of these essentials a man tends to revert, to stop caring much about anything and eventually to let go everything, even his self-respect and healthy pride. All that on the spiritual level, on matters that involve his personality and relationships with his fellows. On the material plane, he tends to gross untidiness, disorder, carelessness about hygiene, personal and otherwise, and general slackness. These things in a crowded ship if left unchecked would lead inevitably to destruction. They can only be countered by discipline, collective and self-imposed; and Henry the Navigator made his ships and their crews the best disciplined the world had so far known. He laid down sanctions for every offence and piece of slackness. Pohl gives a couple of examples. A ship's clerk, he says,

> . . . was liable to branding on the forehead, the loss of his right hand and the forfeiture of his property if he wilfully made a false entry in his book-keeping. A sailor who fell asleep on watch was put on a diet of bread and water; but if the offense should occur in enemy waters, he would be stripped, flogged by his messmates and ducked thrice. If he were an officer, he would have a pail of water flung over his head and water was unpopular in the non-bathing centuries. . . .   [p 104]

With the ships for the job and the right kind of seafarer to man them, Henry now set about his self-imposed task. Finding the country of Prester John was still his main objective; but he now had a subsidiary one besides. A story had become current that seven bishops each with his own wealthy following had taken to the sea in order to evade the advance of the Moors into Portugal and Spain. Rumour had it that they had landed on an island far out in the Ocean and there set up seven separate and prosperous cities. Henry was anxious to locate and establish contact with these saintly refugees who, like their *Island of Seven Cities* and even Prester John, proved in the end to be no more than a myth.

It may seem curious that a man of Henry's proven intelligence and strictly scientific attitude should be taken in by such tales, but one must remember the world in which he lived – how little known it was and how bedevilled by superstition, magic and mysticism. His own ship-masters and pilots were unable to deceive him though they tried hard and long enough.

When the Navigator began his work, the African coast fronting the Atlantic had been explored after a fashion from the Pillars of Hercules south only to Cape Bojador and the Rio de Oro. Beyond that point nobody had penetrated and returned unless one counts Necho's Phoenicians who, if they did make the famous voyage recorded by Herodotus, were travelling the other way round anyhow. This headland, lying only a little way south and east from the Canary Islands, had an awesome reputation and the common belief among seafaring men was that it simply could not be rounded. Expedition after expedition was sent out with orders to push beyond it to the southward and all of them failed. Bojador was the limit, a mystical, magic point beyond which no mere mortal could pass.

That was the story the sailors told; but Henry knew better. He knew his ships were returning loaded with slaves and showing handsome profits on their voyages, and that to do so they had no need to round Bojador. Possibly, being the man he was, he didn't blame them. Neither, however, did he give up. Instead he tried to find the kind of leaders for his expeditions who had vision, far-sighted men who could look beyond immediate gain to an infinitely bigger and more important goal. In doing so he undoubtedly started that process which changed the whole status of seafaring as a

7　Model of Portuguese Caravel at one stage (1536) in its development

profession and over the next three or four centuries lifted it to its apogee. Hitherto the man who followed the sea had been a simple soul without much background, usually a type who didn't fit in anywhere ashore and became a wanderer in consequence. He was clever with his hands, a great improviser and tough, but he lacked culture and the social graces. In 'respectable' company he stood out like a sore thumb or a dirty mark on a white wall and he usually stank of tar, sweat and sour bilge water into the bargain. He was shrewd rather than clever, not over-scrupulous, owed allegiance to few men and no country. Generally speaking he served other interests only when they coincided with his own.

Henry changed all that and cut the ground out from under his scheming shipmasters simply by putting men from his own court, men devoted to him and whom he could trust, in command of the expeditions.

Nevertheless Cape Bojador remained unpassed until twelve years after he first went to Sagres. The man who broke the spell in the end was Henry's squire, Gil Eanes. He was ordered to sail for the dreaded cape and not to return until he had rounded it. Working on a hunch, instead of hugging the shore, he sailed far out to sea and coming back on a wide arc exploded the myth and opened the way not only to the southward but also west into the Atlantic.

That was the beginning and when Henry died in 1460 his seamen had explored and mapped the coastline of West Africa all the way down to Sierra Leone; they had brought home great treasure in the form of slaves and gold-dust; and to crown it all

23

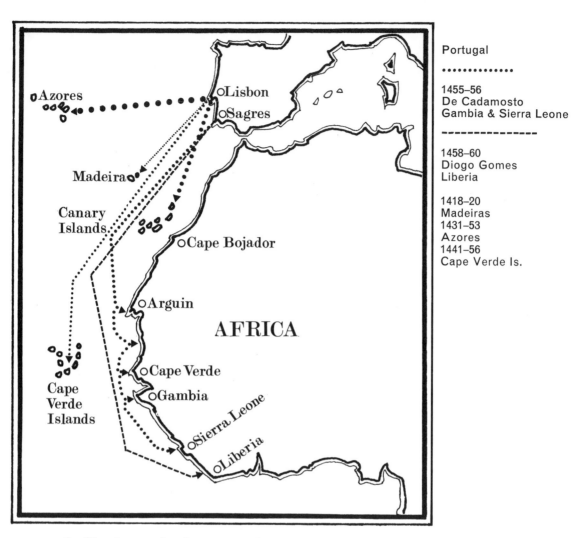

Portugal
· · · · · · · · · · · · ·

1455–56
De Cadamosto
Gambia & Sierra Leone

- - - - - - - - - - - - - - -

1458–60
Diogo Gomes
Liberia

1418–20
Madeiras
1431–53
Azores
1441–56
Cape Verde Is.

8 Sketch-map showing extent of
Portuguese discoveries in Africa at
the time of Henry the
Navigator's death

they had discovered the Cape Verde Islands (1441–56) and not only re-discovered the
Madeiras (1418–20) and the Azores (1431–53) but made them Portuguese for sure by
colonising them.

In the last decade of the Navigator's life there seems to have been an increasing
tendency to play down the religious and mystical element in the voyages he organised
and to concentrate more on trade, the exploitation of new territories and, after the fall
of Constantinople in 1453, on finding the way round Africa not to Prester John's
fabulous kingdom but to the indisputably factual and indispensable spice islands of the
Orient.

It was around this time – in 1454 to be precise – that the first book ever printed
from movable type was published and it is impossible to measure let alone overstate the

ultimate effect of this on the seafarer's life and work. The immediate effect was to release the mathematicians and astronomers, the compilers of portolani and star tables, from their ivory towers and allow them to exchange notes, to discuss, consult and check up on each other in an ever-increasing degree.

2 KING JOHN II (1455-95)

This great advance came too late for the Navigator to make much of it and after his death, the work he had initiated flagged. Lacking a man of his vision and personality to lead them, the Portuguese seamen and shipowners turned to squeezing the most out of what they had got so far. Consequently in the next decade the only voyage sufficiently important to make the records was one under the command of another of Henry's squires, Pedro de Sintra. It was made in two caravels and according to Prestage (*The Portuguese Pioneers*, pp 182 *et seq.*) got round the bulge of the continent as far as Cape Palmas. That was in 1462.

In the meantime a nephew of the Navigator had become king and Prestage says it was seven years after this voyage before he could give attention to the continuance of the work begun by his uncle. When he did so it was along a different line. The main problem now was finding the money to finance these voyages and in 1469 he had the bright idea of farming out the royal rights in the trade of what was now called the Guinea coast to a wealthy citizen of Lisbon named Fernão Gomes. The period of the lease was for five years, the rent 200 *milreis* per annum and among the conditions it was agreed that all the ivory found was to go to the King at a flat rate of 1,500 *reis* the quintal – and Gomes was granted permission to buy one civet-cat each year. In return for all this he was committed to discovering another 100 leagues of coast every twelve months, starting from Sierra Leone.

Gomes knew he was on to a good thing so long as he kept moving and by 1472, using knights of the royal household such as João da Santarem and Pedro de Escolar to command his ships, he had pushed into the Gulf of Guinea and opened up the Gold Coast. His sailing-masters had also found that from Guinea the coast went on to the southward, and another of them, Lopo Gonçalves, pushed on along it to the Equator to be followed in turn by Ruy de Sequeira who finally reached Cape St Catherine, which lies all of 2 degrees south of the Line.

When the contract with Gomes expired in 1474, it was not renewed and it seems obvious that it had become too lucrative for any private individual to be allowed to enjoy. Instead the King, Alfonso V, handed it on to his son John and John, like the Navigator, had ideas. In that same year he caused laws to be passed which first of all made the African trade a crown monopoly and conferred all its revenues upon himself, then prohibited all private enterprises in the seas and islands of Guinea without authorisation. The penalty for breaking this law was quite simply death and confiscation. Private individuals, however, were allowed to sail elsewhere than in the Guinea trade providing they 'first obtained leave and gave security, failing which their ships were to be confiscated. . . .' The idea behind all this was to curb the growing curse of piracy. He also tried to encourage shipbuilding by giving privileges to anybody who built and equipped any craft of more than 100 tons.

Prince John, afterwards to become King John II of Portugal, was according to

Newton ' . . . a very solicitous enquirer into the secrets of the world'. When ship-masters reaching south of the Equator had reported that they were no longer able to fix their latitude by the Pole Star, he immediately got together a panel of mathe-maticians to study the problem. These men who included the Jews Joseph Vizinho and Abraham Zacuto responded by devising a new method of determining latitude from the sun's meridian altitude – that is its height at midday – and made it easier by compiling tables showing the sun's declination.

At last the mariner was beginning to count for something and his contribution to society was not only appreciated but actively and imaginatively encouraged.

Meanwhile Portugal's Catholic neighbour, Spain, was eager to get in on the shipping and discovery racket and even went to war about it. The fighting was largely inconclusive but Portugal's seafaring people got the rough end of it going about their business. Even when it was over the King of Spain still encouraged the seamen of Palos to trade to the Gold Coast; and

> . . . Portugal dared not rely altogether on written agreements and on 6th April 1480 following upon the seizure of a fleet of 35 Spanish merchantmen off Mina, a decree of Alfonso V ordered the crews of foreign vessels found in the sphere granted to him by Papal bulls to be thrown into the sea. . . . [Prestage, p 196]

Portugal continued to do everything in her power to maintain the doctrine of the *mare clausum*, the closed sea, in relation to the Guinea coast and at the same time pushed on to the southward. The next to chance his arm was Diogo Cão who sailed in 1482. Like most of the ship-masters as distinct from the expedition commanders, he came from the lower classes and we can assume he was a bit of a rough-neck. He discovered the mouth of the Congo and went on as far as Cape Lobo in Angola. According to Newton, Diogo Cão travelled farther down the African coast in four years than Henry's seamen had done in forty; but it was still too little and too slow for John, now occupying the throne as John II. In 1487 he sent a member of his court named Covilham to the eastward overland with the avowed purpose of finding the kingdom of Prester John. Of course he failed in this but managed to penetrate as far as Calicut and picked up vital information about the spice trade and the possibilities in it for Portugal.

Covilham's journey casts an oblique but revealing light on the scope of shipping and the pattern of seafaring in the Indian Ocean before the Portuguese got in on it. Accompanied by a man named Paiva, Covilham took ship from Barcelona to Naples and thence to Rhodes, where they bought, and presumably shipped back home, a cargo of honey. From Rhodes they took another ship to Alexandria and then up-river to Cairo. All the time the two men were enquiring, recording and making contacts among merchants and traders. They finally linked up with a party of Moors and in the spring of 1488 got aboard a small Arab craft bound to Aden via Suakin. At Aden the two men parted, Paiva heading for Ethiopia and Covilham for India, aboard a 'Mecca ship' of 200 or 300 tons burden. The Monsoon was favourable and they made Cananor in a month. From there he went on to Calicut which was the richest port in India and the centre of the spice trade. Arrivals and sailings were governed by the Monsoon:

> In August and September ships from Aden and the Straits arrived with goods from the West, and in February they left for home with pepper, cloves, cinnamon, rhubarb, precious stones, porcelain and other merchandise which had been brought to Calicut from other parts of India and from Ceylon and the Far East. . . . [Prestage, p 219]

9 Portuguese fort at Mina on West African Coast. From a book
by Oliver Dapper, dated Amsterdam 1670

Covilham, having picked up all he could single-handed in Calicut, began working his way to the north. He looked in at Goa, at that time the centre of a trade in horses which were shipped across the Arabian Sea as cavalry remounts for the armies of various Indian potentates; then crossed the Persian Gulf to Ormuz – a great haunt of traders – and took ship to Sofala on the African coast. The commodity dealt in here was gold brought down from the mines in the interior and, after a good look at it, Covilham headed back to Aden where he arrived in October 1490. With four years wandering behind him he got as far as Cairo homeward bound and there learned that Paiva had died in his search for Prester John. He was advised of this in a message from John II which added that he was not to rest until this part of his mission had been accomplished. Taskmasters were truly hard and demanding in those days! Nevertheless it can be assumed that Covilham was content for after another three years of travelling he got to Abyssinia and, settling down at last, lived there for thirty years.

3 BARTOLOMEO DIAS (*c.* 1455–1500)

While Covilham was feeling his way eastward, King John II continued his groping southward down the Atlantic coast of the African continent. In August 1486 he launched the expedition which was to bring undying fame to the Portuguese seafarer in the name of Bartolomeo Dias. It consisted of two caravels of about 50 tons each and a store-ship of a size and rig unknown but presumably smaller than the others. The store-ship was the answer to the food problem. She was loaded with provisions and the idea was to leave her somewhere along the route as a depot at which they could replenish their stores for the passage home. Dias was the leader of the venture and according to Prestage he was 'a knight of the royal household'. He commanded the flagship with Pero de Alenquer as pilot and a seaman called Leitão as master; and from here on, be it noted, the separation of the function of command from the more technical responsibilities of navigation and actual sailing becomes more marked. The second ship was the *St Pantaleão*. She too was commanded by a knight of the household, a man named John Infante with Alvaro Martins as his pilot and John Grego for sailing-master. The store-ship was under the command of Pedro Dias, a brother of Bartolomeo, and he had with him John de Santiago, pilot, and John Alves, master.

There is no official report of the voyage and the existing descriptions of it are not wholly reliable or consistent but it seems fairly certain Dias finally left Lisbon in August 1487. It would appear discovery was not his only objective and he was concerned also with what is known in the modern idiom as 'showing the flag' for the sake of the lucrative Guinea trade. Newton estimates that the profits in this from gold-dust alone ran at around 170,000 gold doubloons a year. To foster and enhance this fabulous traffic Dias:

> . . . carried two negroes who Cao had seized and taken to Portugal and four negresses from the Guinea coast, who were landed at various places on the coast, well dressed and supplied with samples of silver, gold and spices. These they were to take inland and shew and at the same time proclaim the greatness of Portugal. . . .   [Prestage, p 223]

There was a Portuguese fort now at Mina in the Gulf of Guinea and trading posts would have been set up a long way to the south of that in the wake of Diogo Cão, so the first part of the voyage presented no difficulty. Newton suggests Dias ran straight on past the mouth of the Congo to Port Alexander where he landed his negroes and left the store-ship. According to Prestage it was south of that in Walfisch Bay that he parted company with her, but the difference is unimportant. What matters is that somewhere south of Walfisch Bay he encountered head-winds which drove him off the land and, before he could regain it, shifted to become strong northerly gales. There was nothing he could do about it but run, and run he did, always to the southward for thirteen cold, wet, weary days.

It is difficult now, almost impossible to imagine what went on in the minds of the men aboard those two ships. Captain Bligh of the *Bounty* might have known in his day and perhaps Sir Ernest Shackleton too after his open boat passage from Elephant Island to South Georgia, but only in part, for they both knew where they were heading while Bartolomeo's men hadn't a clue. The gale was driving them deeper and deeper into the latitudes known to sailing ship men as the 'roaring forties'. There the seas run higher and wilder than anywhere else in the world. They start up somewhere to the west of Cape Horn and never finish for there is nothing to stop them or damp them down in all the complete circuit of the globe; and these Portuguese tarpaulins were the first men ever to see them. They watched and saw them grow higher day by day while overhead the grey sky with the mad wind screaming out of it became more sullen, more menacing, and the cold crept hour by hour deeper into their bones.

To sustain them they had a meagre diet of salt-fish, dried goat's flesh and maggoty biscuits probably varied on Sundays only by a little sour wine instead of slimy green water to wash it down with. In such cramped quarters as the ships provided, their physical deterioration must have been frighteningly rapid but not nearly so terrifying as the sight of the endless empty sea and the mounting superstitious dread of where it was taking them.

There is no telling how long they could have endured or even how they would have broken in the end, but fortunately they were not called on to face that ultimate test and as soon as the wind allowed it Bartolomeo got his ships round and headed east. Obviously he expected the land to lift above the horizon almost immediately and when it didn't he hoisted more sail and pressed on, driving ships and men for all they were worth. The first day passed, and the next, and the one after that, and still the longed-for land did not appear. Spirits began to flag again and all the superstitious fears came crowding back in on the baffled, bewildered seamen; and then 'after some days' the commander began to understand what had happened. Working out in his own mind that by pure blind chance he had rounded the southern tip of the African continent, he headed north and after sailing 150 leagues* on this new course sighted mountains to prove it. He ran in and on 3 February 1488 anchored in what is now known as Mossel Bay. Dias called it *Bahia dos Vaqueiros* because cows were being herded on the beach there and a welcome sight they must have been. Assuming it was the end of August when he left Lisbon and that his stays at Port Alexander and in Walfisch Bay were brief, the passage had occupied over 150 days.

Dias himself had no inclination to linger there and in spite of murmurings among his crews he pressed on along the coast as far as the Great Fish River. There, however, he was compelled to yield to the entreaties and demands of his seamen and turn back. The men were worn out with exposure, deprivation and mental strain, and feared if they went on any farther all of them would perish. It must have been desperately

*A league at this time was the equivalent of about three modern English miles.

Portugal

● ● ● ● ● ●

Bartolomeo Dias

1487
1 Lisbon
2 Congo
3 Cape Cross
4 Cabo da Volta
5 Cape of Good Hope
6 Mossel Bay
7 Great Fish River
1488

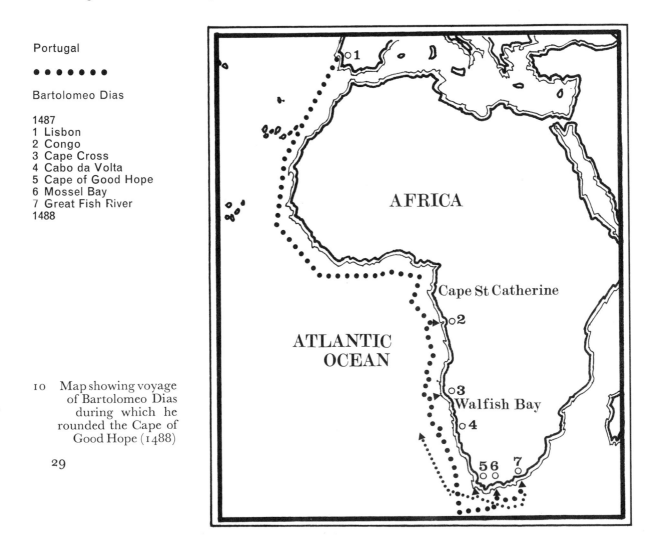

10 Map showing voyage of Bartolomeo Dias during which he rounded the Cape of Good Hope (1488)

29

difficult for Dias to give up his quest at this stage when he had already achieved so much and all the rest of it lay right before him; but he was obviously a wise commander who knew when to stop. His disappointment is recorded by the early chroniclers like Barros. By rising above it and bowing to the inevitable he proved he had the kind of strength that makes a good seaman.

The passage home was longer than the one out. On the way he sighted the southern tip of the continent and the story is that he called it the Stormy Cape; but King John would have none of that and 'changed the name to that of *Cape of Good Hope*, because it gave promise of the discovery of India, which had been sought for so many years'. After that he headed for his store-ship and rejoined her 270 days after the parting. There had been nine men aboard her but only three survived, and another story is that one of these 'died of pleasure at the sight of his companions'. The store-ship was unloaded into the caravels and then abandoned and burnt, and Dias made a leisurely passage northward, calling at Mina for a load of gold-dust with which presumably to pay his expenses. He reached home in December 1488.

Prestage says there are no authentic portraits of Dias and that nothing is known of his personality or of the reward he received for this great voyage; but there is no doubt of its importance, for it demonstrated beyond all doubt the feasibility of the sea-route to India and Vasco da Gama's voyage was founded on it. More than that, Bartolomeo Dias was engaged to superintend the construction and equipment of the ships built for that enterprise and furnished da Gama with much valuable information about the winds and ways of the South Atlantic.

4 VASCO DA GAMA (1469–1524)

Before anything could be done about using the gateway to the East which Bartolomeo Dias had prised open, King John II, known now as the *Perfect*, was dead, being succeeded in 1495 by Manoel the Fortunate. Powerful arguments were adduced against pursuing the quest dreamed up by Henry the Navigator all those years back. They were mainly political and economic and balanced by a correspondingly powerful urge to counter the current Spanish discoveries to the west. In the end, the King, who favoured the project, ordered it to be got under way and vested the leadership of the new expedition in Vasco da Gama, a gentleman of his household who was already being groomed for the job in the previous reign.

As with Dias, little is known of his background and early life; but it has been established that he had some training in naval matters and some technical knowledge of navigation. One of the main tasks of the expedition, however, would be to establish diplomatic as well as commercial relations with the rulers of India and it was his potential as an ambassador as much or more than his qualifications as a navigator that got him the job.

There were four ships to his fleet: the *St Gabriel*, commanded by da Gama with Pero de Alenquer as pilot or navigator; the *St Raphael* with da Gama's brother Paul in command and a pilot named John de Coimbra; the *Berrio* captained by Nicolas Coelho and navigated by Pero de Escolar; and a store-ship of which the name has been lost. Quite a lot is known about the lines and rig of these ships from a coloured drawing in a 16th-century MS. called *Memoria das Armadas* preserved at the Lisbon Academy of

11 Manoel the Fortunate, King of
Portugal (1469–1521)

12 Vasco da Gama. From a panel
in the hall of the Viceroy's
palace at Goa dated 1547

Sciences; and it is generally agreed that the *St Gabriel* and *St Raphael* were three-masted ships, square-rigged and designed to draw relatively little water so they could operate safely among the shoals and sandbanks of the African coast. The record puts their tonnage at from 100 to 120 but this figure is largely meaningless now, the method of measurement in those days being quite different. The experts appear to think that the figures could be doubled without exaggerating too much. J. Holland Rose says the *St Gabriel* was 84 feet long and carried over 4,000 square feet of canvas. The ships were square-sterned with castles both fore and aft and 'they bore a figure of their patron saint at the bow'. The *Berrio* is described as a 'lateen-rigged caravel of the class used in the Henrician expeditions', and her size is quoted as 50 tons. The store-ship at 200 tons seems to have been the jumbo of the fleet.*

   The ships were armed with twenty guns and while the officers wore armour and carried swords, the ratings were dressed in leather jerkins and breastplates, and furnished with cross-bows, axes and pikes. In the holds were loaded trade goods and various types of merchandise to be used as gifts, and the *Roteiro* criticises the choice

*Most of these details come from the *Roteiro*, a record composed by Alvaro Velho, a member of the expedition. It was first printed in 1838 and subsequently translated by E. G. Ravenstein to be published by the Hakluyt Society in 1898.

31

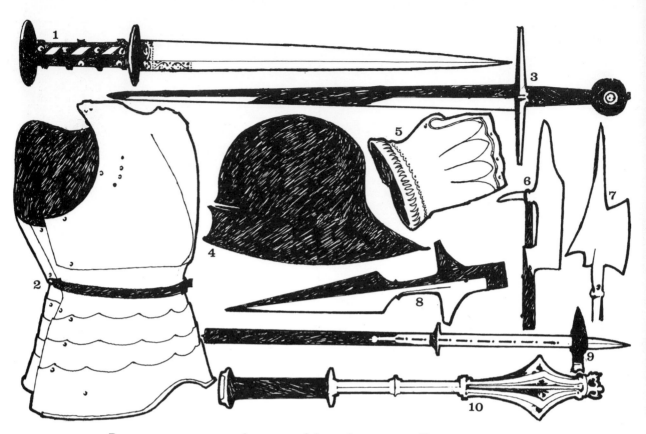

13   Portuguese weapons and armour of the 15th century. 1 Dagger;
2 Cuirass; 3 Sword; 4 Sallet; 5 Gauntlet; 6 and 7 Halberds;
8 Spear; 9 War Hammer; 10 Mace

saying the former were unsuitable for the Indian market and the presents were not nearly rich enough to please or impress the eastern rulers surrounded as they were with magnificence. According to Prestage:

> Ignorance explains the first mistake, but not altogether the second; King Manoel had large commitments and would not spend money without good hope of return; the expedition had cost him a large amount and the issue of the voyage was doubtful. [p 251]

One wonders now what else was skimped and how many more crew members would have survived if no expense had really been spared.

So far as charts, instruments and astronomical tables went the provision was lavish, while a priest was allocated to each ship together with a group of convicts to do the dirty work and try out the risk involved in anything or any place unknown. In all the expedition mustered 170 men.

The captains were summoned before the King for a final briefing and there was a great deal of impressive ceremony with a white silk banner bearing the cross of the Order of Christ; but although His Majesty talked of spreading the Christian faith he also openly declared that he was demanding the discovery of India in order 'to acquire the riches of the East'.

Da Gama sailed from the Tagus on 8 July 1497 and if the scenes at his departure

32

as described by Barros are any guide, the onlookers took a very poor view of his chance of returning.

> . . . while the sails were being unfurled some of the crowd commended the mariners to God, while others gave their opinions about the expedition. . . .   [Prestage, p 252]

It would seem the populace in general deplored the hazardous journey and could see no good coming out of it for anybody. As it turned out they were right at least so far as those directly involved were concerned though the ultimate benefit to mankind is incalculable.

So Vasco da Gama sailed and quite early on it began to look as if he had a jinx with him. He made good time to the Canaries, then the ships lost each other in a fog, suffered some damage to spars and rigging in a gale and met up again at the Cape Verde Islands eighteen days out from Lisbon. By and large that is quite fast going for those days. After a week at anchor making repairs and replenishing provisions, they got going again on 3 August, making a south-easterly course. Again bad weather was encountered and again the *St Gabriel* was damaged, this time breaking her mainyard, and spending two days hove-to while it was being repaired. Getting under way again da Gama now acted on the experience and advice of Bartolomeo Dias, and instead of hugging the coast he headed out south and west into the unknown Atlantic on what afterwards became the recognised route for sailing ships bound for the Cape of Good Hope. The course makes the most of the prevailing winds and currents but ships have been unlucky on it and da Gama, the pioneer, was the unluckiest of them all, except that he survived. They had covered 4,300 miles and it was ninety-six days – three whole months and a week – after leaving St Thiago in the Cape Verdes before they sighted land again, and the fortitude, the endurance, the faith in themselves and their commander – the unvarnished guts of these men – take the breath away. Subsequently the passage was often surpassed for duration. In the 19th century 100 days was a reasonably quick run out to Australia and in the early 1920s the barque *Janes*, bound from South Shields to Mauritius with a cargo of fire-bricks for ballast, was 154 days from her departure at the Lizard to her next landfall, which was made on that tropical island's coast. In all that time she had sighted neither land nor other ship; but the circumstances were different. Her crew had lime-juice as a sure counter to scurvy, tinned provisions including condensed milk as well as salt beef and pork; they had a reliable chronometer with which to calculate their longitude and always they knew more or less where they were and where they were going. They knew for sure. Not so da Gama's men. They were pushing into the blue emptiness with no certainty of being able to get back and every mile of southing and westing they made must have demanded a very special kind of courage from them.

Da Gama's landfall was on the African coast and sailing south along it they came after three more days to a bay which he named Santa Helena. Here he laid up to clean the ships' bottoms, to do a few running repairs and to take the opportunity of making precise observations with the astrolabe. When worked up into latitude and averaged his sights put him barely thirty leagues from the Cape and it is reckoned he was only two leagues out.

The little fleet got going again on 16 November but the jinx was still riding them. They sighted the Cape on the 18th but head-winds prevented them rounding it until the 22nd. Still, round it they did and on the 25th they anchored in Mossel Bay. Another

33

thirteen days were spent here during which time the store-ship was unloaded into the other vessels and, when she was empty, broken up. It will be remembered that Bartolomeo Dias also destroyed his store-ship when the time came to abandon her. No reason has so far been put forward for them doing this and it seems a curiously perverse and futile act of destruction. It could have been done to cover up their tracks or merely to avoid any possibility of helping any grasping Spaniard or rapacious Englishman who might conceivably follow in their wake; for as has been shown they believed in the *mare clausum* and wanted it all for themselves.

With the crews thoroughly refreshed the voyage was continued on 8 December, which was the Feast of the Immaculate Conception. Almost immediately they encountered more heavy weather and so terrifying were the seas that Barros declares 'the danger of shipwreck was such that the crews thought more of bewailing their sins than of attending to the navigation'. Nevertheless the Great Fish River – Bartolomeo Dias's farthest east – was passed in eight days and by Christmas Day they had reached seventy leagues beyond it and come to a land they named Natal.

Again they pushed on, struggling against adverse currents and suffering more hardship, this time from shortage of water, but steadily working northwards and spurred on by the prospect of an early contact with the East African Moslems. Da Gama had a definite target in his sights now – five of them in fact. They were places well known from the reports of overland travellers like Covilham. Sofala, just south of present-day Beira, was one and the best bet. The others were Mozambique, Kilwa, Mombasa and Malindi. For some reason he failed to make Sofala, passing far to the eastward of it, but on 25 January he arrived off Kilimane.

This in effect was the link-up by sea of East and West that Henry the Navigator had conceived in the beginning of the century and spent the rest of his life trying to bring about. There is no record of what Vasco da Gama felt about the long-term implications but it is certain that any elation or sense of triumph in him was tempered by what followed. The mariners were well received by the people of Kilimane and stayed-over there for thirty-two days, careening their ships and refitting. It should have been a wonderful holiday for the sea-weary crews, a time of rejoicing and gladness. Instead the whole period was saddened by sickness and death among them: '. . . many of the crews fell ill and some died of scurvy', says Prestage. The scourge must have already struck the ships while on passage because the onset of scurvy is never sudden and the death it brings is a slow one. The leader's brother, Paul da Gama, acquired a reputation for great kindness at this point by 'visiting the sick and distributing among them the medicines he had brought for his own use'. In this can already be sensed that gulf between officers and foremast hands which has persisted in ships till modern times and in living memory was manifested among other ways by a different scale and quality of provision for each; *cabin* biscuits and hard-tack or Liverpool pantiles, *cabin* tea and *crew* coffee, hash in the mess-rooms forward and curried prawns with mango chutney in the saloon amidships, Board of Trade minimum measured out *pound and pint* in the fo'c'sles and *full and plenty* aft.

Quoting a contemporary source, Prestage gives the daily rations of food and drink issued to the crews of da Gama's ships as:

Biscuit	1½ lb	Water	2½ pints
Beef	1 lb	Wine	1½ pints
or Pork	½ lb	plus oil and vinegar.	

This compares quite favourably with the standard rations issued in the British Navy up to 1939 which are listed in the *Manual of Seamanship*, vol. 1 as follows:

Bread	10 ozs	Condensed milk	¾ oz
Beef or Mutton, frozen	½ lb	Jam, Pickles or Marmalade	1 oz
Vegetables or	1 lb	Corned beef on one day a week	
Beans or Peas when potatoes not		in harbour or twice a week at	
available	4 ozs	sea	4 ozs
Sugar	2 ozs	Mustard, pepper, salt and vine-	
Chocolate	½ oz	gar as required	

but it should be noted that a Messing Allowance was paid in addition to the standard ration.

How many died in Kilimane is not recorded but it was only the beginning of the losses and in the end only a third – 55 out of 170 according to Rose – of the original company survived to see home again.

The next stop was Mozambique where the little fleet arrived on 2 March. Here again the Portuguese were well received although subsequent events suggest the friendliness was either a front or inspired by fear of the ships' guns. Anyhow

> ... the natives came on board freely and partook of Portuguese hospitality. Through an interpreter da Gama heard that they traded with Arabs, four of whose vessels, laden with gold, silver, jewels and spices, were then in the port, that these commodities abounded farther on, so that there was no need to purchase them and that precious stones could be collected in baskets! ... [Prestage, pp 256–7]

and such confirmation that they were on the track of untold wealth which could be had merely for the trouble of taking it must have offset a lot of the commander's grief for his dead seamen.

The ships in the port are described by the *Roteiro* but only in vague general terms; nothing precise. They were, he tells us, 'large and decked, but had no nails, the planks being held together by cords. ....' But there is no mention of length and beam, nor of the rig, though he does say the sails were made of palm-matting, and adds that the vessels were equipped with mariner's compass, quadrant and charts. It could be that what he took for sails were in fact awnings.

Da Gama's big idea now was to counter the perils of a coast unknown to him by shipping a local pilot. In the event he got two, but one deserted and the other, after being flogged for some offence, betrayed him. Instead of taking the ships in to Kilwa he went on to Mombasa where a plot to capture them by force had been cooked up by the Sultan. By pure chance the scheme was discovered in time to foil it but from then on there was an end to all pretence of friendship and nobody trusted anybody any more. Deep down the antagonism was rooted in religious difference but there is no doubt it was aggravated by the stupidly brutal way in which the Portuguese reacted to it. Besides beating up the pilot as already mentioned they 'put to the torture' certain citizens of Mozambique in order to squeeze out of them information about the ruler's intentions, and were in general very high-handed and arrogant in their dealings with the Moslems.

In the short term the tough line paid off for when da Gama reached Malindi on 14 April the ruler did everything possible to appease him, putting on fêtes and side-shows and making ceremonial gifts of live sheep and valuable spices. Nevertheless he

35

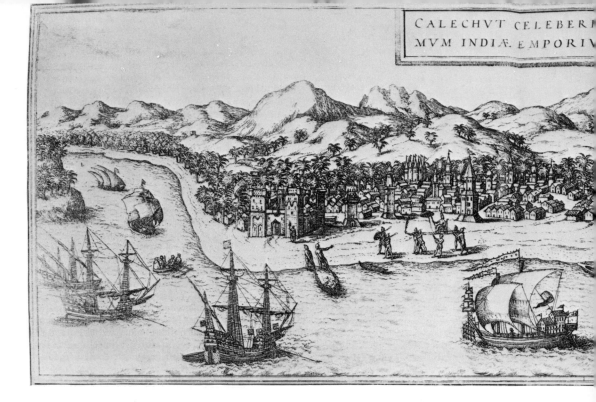

stuck in his toes about providing a pilot and in the end gave way only to obtain the release of a favourite servant who was being forcibly detained by the Portuguese commander.

Thus was blackmail added to flogging and torture in Vasco da Gama's record, which already describes him as irascible and even violent at times; but he got his pilot – a Guzerati named Ibn Majid – and on 24 April he pushed on towards Calicut. This leg was the least demanding of the whole passage, if only because one man in the fleet – the pilot – had been that way before and knew where he was heading. It lasted just over three weeks and they made their Asian landfall, the first ever by a European ship, on 18 May. Two days later they anchored outside Calicut and Henry the Navigator's dream had come true.

The Moslem traders in Calicut were quick to see that the possibility of Portugal cutting herself in on the Indian markets was a threat to their special interests and da Gama got only a dusty welcome. In fact, although he acquired a great deal of valuable information and established some useful contacts, in the end he was lucky ever to get out of the place. A less suspicious, guarded and shrewd commander might well have lost his ships there and his own life into the bargain. As it was, he avoided all the traps set for him and even obtained a small consignment of spices, then at the end of August upped anchor and sailed for home.

Again the luck was all against him and with calms and head-winds keeping him backing and filling all the way across the Arabian Sea it was not until 3 January 1499 that he made his landfall on the African coast just north of the Equator near Mogadishu. On the 7th he put into Malindi and by then he had lost another thirty of his men by scurvy, and the rest were so weakened by the disease that 'only seven or eight men in each ship were fit for duty'.

Cutting his losses, he divided his surviving hands between the *St Gabriel* and the

36

14   Harbour at Calicut (early 16th century)

Berrio and burned the *St Raphael* – again that seemingly senseless destruction of a ship that might well have been the difference between life and death for somebody following in his wake. Curiously or superstitiously he saved the figure-head and carted it home. According to Prestage it can still be seen in the Jerónimos Church at Belém.

The luck remained against da Gama and it seems as if he had to fight for every yard of the way home. On 1 February he reached Mozambique and the two surviving ships rounded the Cape together on 20 March. A month later they were still struggling to the northward. Then they parted company involuntarily in a storm and the *Berrio*, still with Coelho in command, finally made the River Tagus on 10 July, two years and two days after leaving it.

Meanwhile the flagship had put in at St Thiago in the Cape Verdes with the commander's kindly brother Paul mortally sick. Vasco da Gama is supposed to have sent the *St Gabriel* on from there while he took Paul in a chartered caravel to Terceira in the Azores. There the brother died and Vasco arrived back in Lisbon on 9 September, making a triumphal entry nine days later.

As a diplomatic mission the voyage was a failure but in other ways a very great success. Prestage sums it up as follows:

. . . he had found India, and brought back samples of its products – cinnamon, cloves, ginger, nutmeg, pepper and precious stones. What he had accomplished could be repeated, for the first step is always the most difficult and fabulous wealth lay open to Portugal if only she had the courage to seize it. His voyage out was the finest feat of seamanship recorded up to that time and greater than that of Columbus, for not only had the latter a much shorter distance to travel, but, favoured by the wind, he could proceed almost straight from the Canaries to his goal. . . .   [p 266]

His courses and discoveries were charted with remarkable accuracy compared with, for instance, those of Columbus who was liable to be as much as 10 degrees out

37

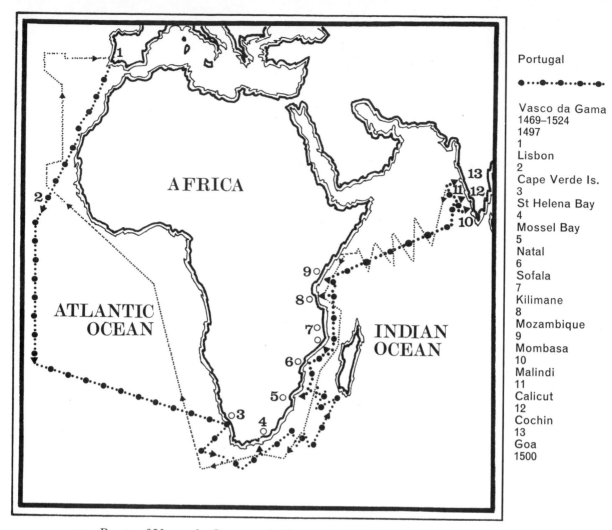

15   Route of Vasco da Gama to India
      and his return

even in his latitude; and altogether his contribution to the development of seafaring was surpassed by very few men indeed. The voyage weakened Islam politically by establishing an arrogant, thrusting power on its flank and economically by skimming off the cream of the Oriental trade at the expense of Moslem traders. Finally it led to the establishment of an overseas empire for Portugal and gave her in the end a virtual monopoly of the spice trade.

King Manoel reacted by adding another to his string of titles, declaring himself *Lord of the conquest, navigation and commerce of Ethiopia, Arabia, Persia and India.*

And if one is asked what was in it for Vasco da Gama, the answer is plenty. He was given the title of *Dom*, a pension of 1000 *cruzados* per annum and the town of Vidigueira to lord it over, to start with; then in 1519 he was made Count Vidigueira, given an additional pension, the title of *Admiral of the Indian Seas* and the right to import merchandise from the East to the value of 200 *cruzados*, which made him one of the richest men in Portugal. His last job for the crown was Viceroy of India and he died in

1524. On what was in it for those who died of scurvy on the voyage or their dependants the record is silent except that the foremast hands were paid five *cruzados* a month, the carpenter, caulker and other tradesmen, seven. The King himself, it is said, gave 'married men 100 *cruzados* each to leave with their wives and 40 to single men'.

5 PEDRO ALVARES CABRAL (*c.* 1460–*c.* 1526)

Manoel knew now he was on to a good thing and he lost no time in playing it up for all it was worth. Another Indian voyage was organised with all possible speed – a bigger and better one with thirteen ships and heavier armed. Among the personnel selected for the trip were Bartolomeo Dias, Nicolas Coelho and Duarte Pacheco, three of the most experienced navigators of the day. The ships were stored for an eighteen months voyage and sailed from Lisbon on 9 March 1500 under the command of Pedro Alvares Cabral.

This time the seamen were signed on for 10 *cruzados* a month and given the right to bring home ten quintals of pepper each for his own profit. Married men had a year's pay in advance and the single ones six months. Was it the risk of scurvy that was pushing up the market price of their services?

The fleet made fast time and was among the Canary Islands by the 14th and sighted the Cape Verdes on the 22nd. Steering west and south into the Atlantic like his predecessors, and losing one of his fleet on the way, Cabral raised the coast of South America on 22 April and, naming the land *Vera Cruz* (True Cross), claimed it for Portugal.

There is some doubt as to whether this discovery was either as accidental or original as it was made out to be. Some authorities suggest Brazil had been found as far back as 1494 but because of political considerations connected with the rivalry of Spain and the Treaty of Tordesillas (which shall be dealt with in a later section) Manoel was keeping the discovery up his sleeve as a strong card to be played at an appropriate time. According to these commentators, Cabral had secret instructions to go there and make the discovery official. At that time the place was believed to be a big island though this was quickly disproved by subsequent voyagers.

Cabral remained on the coast of Brazil until 2 May, then headed out on a course that would take him south of the Cape of Good Hope into the Indian Ocean. He had reduced his fleet to ten ships now and he made better time than da Gama but paid for progress in the grimmest possible way. In a sudden squall when they were three weeks out from Vera Cruz, four of his vessels were overwhelmed and went down with all hands. Among them was that commanded by Bartolomeo Dias, who thus evaded old bones and a slow death in somebody else's chimney corner by making a sailor's end.

Pursued and battered by wild weather all the way, the six remaining ships reached Sofala on 16 July. They were then seventy-five days out from the Brazilian coast and must have been badly worn and near exhaustion; but Cabral showed no inclination to linger, and, pressing on, he came to Mozambique on the 20th and to Kilwa on the 26th. His welcome at both these places was distinctly cool. They were looked on as pirates and nobody would do business with them. Consequently he went on to Malindi and there managed to get a Guzerati pilot for the passage across the Indian Ocean. Reaching the Laccadive Islands on 22 August they stayed over for fifteen days to water

16 The Jerónimos Monastery at Belém, by H. l'Eveque, 1816. The
monastery was built by Manoel to commemorate the
discovery of the sea route to India. Vasco da Gama was
buried here. Also shown is the bar of the River Tagus with
lateen-rigged craft in foreground and the three-masters beyond

and rest the crews, and on 13 September arrived at Calicut, 188 days out from Lisbon;
and this for a very long time to come was reckoned to be the usual length of a voyage
to India via the Cape.

The reputation of the Portuguese was spreading and their ready resort to such
persuasive gimmicks as thumbscrews and garotte, cat and bastinado, did nothing to
sweeten it; nor were there any illusions about their aims and ends. Consequently
their welcome at Calicut was no warmer than it had been on the East African coast.
But profiting from da Gama's experience, Cabral used a different approach. Taking a
tough line from the start, he grabbed off a number of hostages and then proceeded to
separate the ruler – called the Samuri – from the Moslem merchants. Loading the
potentate with rich presents he managed to convince him that whatever happened to
anybody else he himself would profit from trade with the Portuguese. After three
months of fast talk and lavish sweetening, the Samuri gave orders that cargoes were to
be found for the ships of the strangers. In the event, however, only two ships were
loaded, which caused the ruler to stop the stowing of all Moorish vessels until Cabral's
remaining four were full.

By this time the ruler was so completely in Cabral's pocket that he gave him
authority to stop and search Moorish vessels and seize any carrying spices. On 16
December the Portuguese arrogantly used this authority and seized a ship sailing from
the port. The Moslems in the place thereupon attacked the *factory* (or warehouse) which
Cabral had established and killed the factor and fifty of his men. The Portuguese
commander retaliated by seizing ten Moslem ships, appropriating their cargoes,
slaughtering their crews and bombarding the city.

Honour having thus been served, an adequate eye extracted and tooth kicked in for every one of each lost, and the heathens taught a lesson they would not quickly forget, Cabral went on to Cochin and Cananor to complete his loading with pepper at the first place and ginger at the other. His passage home was uneventful except for the quiet discovery of the island of St Helena on the way, though some authorities credit this to John da Nova on a subsequent voyage. He arrived in Lisbon on 23 June 1501 and though half of his fleet had been lost, the venture still showed a handsome profit.

With a shrewd eye on the main chance, King Manoel had already concluded that to obtain the maximum profit from the eastern trade the voyages in that direction must be regular and continuous. The three already made, counting that of Bartolomeo Dias, had demonstrated that weather-wise there was a right time and a wrong one for starting. By sailing in the month of March, a ship would make better time southward to the Cape and catch a fair wind for the long haul north and east across the Indian Ocean. He decided to make the sailings an annual event and while Cabral was still in transit had sent out John da Nova with four ships. Not much is known about this voyage except that the ships all got back safely in September 1502 with cargoes of spices.

Meanwhile in Lisbon there was no criticism of Cabral's strong-arm tactics. Nor in view of the size of the profits being made could there be any question of discontinuing the voyages just because the natives and the Moslems were hostile to them; but if the trade was to prosper and flourish the time had come to read the recalcitrants a lesson, and the man chosen for the task was Vasco da Gama.

He sailed in February 1502 with a fleet of fifteen ships later supplemented by another five that sailed in April. The purpose of the expedition was threefold. First it was to punish all those who had been hostile to the Portuguese voyagers all the way from Sofala to Cananor; next it was to strengthen and protect the Portuguese factories already established on the Indian coast and harry Moslem shipping heading for the Red Sea; and finally it was to bring home the biggest cargo of spices ever known.

Da Gama did not spare himself and pulled no punches. Starting at Kilwa, where he squeezed 2000 *maticals* of gold out of the Sultan (afterwards used to make a monstrance for the Church of Jerónimos at Belém), he left a wide wake of mourning behind him all the way to Calicut. Male or female, young or old – the Moslems were all the same to him and he wiped them out indiscriminately wherever he encountered them. One of his grimmest exploits was to set fire to a ship full of pilgrims returning from Mecca and he brought war to the coast of India, bombarding the city of Calicut and sinking all the ships sent out to try and stop him.

There have been apologists for da Gama. Prestage says of him:

. . . The acts of frightfulness committed by him and some of his successors may perhaps apart from the cruelty of those times and the lust for revenge, be explained by the fact that the Portuguese were a mere handful of men at a year's distance from home, among hundreds of thousands of actual and potential foes. It was probably felt that these had to be cowed for safety's sake. . . .   [p 294]

Moreover in modern times man's inhumanity to man has reached such terrifying depths that the 15th-century Portuguese begin to look like small-time operators against the 20th-century product. But that hardly justifies them nor does it add any lustre to their laurels.

6 ALFONSO D'ALBUQUERQUE (1453–1515)

Portugal was set now on the naked conquest of the East but curiously her next commander acquired a reputation for wisdom and humanity. He was Alfonso d'Albuquerque, another courtier turned seafarer out of ambition, greed or plain lust for power or maybe a bit of all three. Born in 1453 near Lisbon Albuquerque has been called the founder of Portuguese power in the East. He sailed in 1503, presumably in the spring, with two squadrons of ships, the second in command of his cousin, Francisco. They were joined a year later by another fleet numbering thirteen ships under the command of Lopo Soares de Meneses.

By a lucky chance Albuquerque was able to win the gratitude and friendship of the Rajah of Cochin almost immediately he arrived on the coast. With this kind of backing he soon established factories and raised forts for their protection at various points.

And now the story, up to this point reasonably clear and simple, begins to be confused and involved. King Manoel was not content with one string to his bow nor was he inclined to wait for events to develop. He wanted action and set out to get it. The consequences of the Portuguese thrust into the spice trade, both economic and political, were already becoming manifest not only in Mecca and Egypt but also in Venice and as far afield as northern Europe. Spices were reaching Antwerp through Portugal as early as 1501 and the trade was so lucrative that German and Italian firms with copper to export to India set up warehouses and offices in Lisbon. The European monopoly in the spice trade hitherto held by Venice was broken and the prosperity of the great city-state began to decline. Seeing the writing clear upon the wall, Venice entered into some kind of agreement with the Sultan of Egypt who was also losing heavily in transit dues because of the Portuguese diversion of spice cargoes round the Cape. The Sultan threatened to destroy the Holy Places in Palestine unless the Indian voyages were abandoned and efforts were made to get the Pope to ban them. Manoel's reaction was the decision to make his control of the spice trade an absolute monopoly and to maintain it with a large and permanent military force in the East.

17 The Return of the Ambassadors by Carpaccio. This picture illustrates vividly the opulence of 15th-century Venice

18   An attack on Aden from the sea by the Portuguese, as seen in
an anonymous Flemish woodcut. That made by Albuquerque
in 1513 was unsuccessful

In March 1504 he dispatched a convoy of twenty-two ships under the command
of a grandee called Don Francisco de Almeida. The fleet included merchant vessels
belonging to several German trading firms and carried a total of 2,500 men of whom
1,500 were plain, unvarnished soldiers. Nothing is recorded of the purely nautical
aspects of the voyage out and it can be assumed that in spite of the hazards and torments
the passage round the Cape had by this time become something of a commonplace.
The main concern of Almeida was to safeguard the route by setting up forts at strategic
points on the East African coast and the one he built at Kilwa was 'so strong that it
would keep even the King of France at bay'. He also attacked and destroyed Mombasa
to teach the inhabitants respect for the white man and his religion.

Arrived on the coast of India Almeida declared himself Viceroy and set up a kind
of government at Cochin. Then, still flourishing his military might at the least sign of
resistance, he got control of Ceylon which was the source of the world's cinnamon
supply.

Lisbon had now superseded Venice as the centre of the spice trade and Prestage
lists among the items dealt in:

> . . . pepper, ginger, cinnamon, mace, cloves and nutmeg; while the principal drugs were
> red sandal-wood, verzin, wormwood, mastic, spikenard, borax, camphor, rhubarb, aloes,
> musk and civet.   [p 297]

He adds that Portuguese ships landed a large cargo of spices at Falmouth in 1504,
but the distributing centre for northern Europe was the depot set up by John II at
Antwerp some years before that.

43

Pursuing the consolidating element in Manoel's policy, Tristão da Cunha in 1506 cleaned up the coast of Madagascar and took over an Arab fort on the island of Socotra which they thought would dominate the entrance to the Red Sea. This was later abandoned, for Aden was the real key and rendered Socotra ineffective. At the same time Alfonso de Albuquerque grabbed off Ormuz wherewith to overlook the Persian Gulf.

With the long lines of communication secure the way was clear now for further expansion and Albuquerque was the man who saw to it. Succeeding Almeida as Viceroy in 1509 he ruled the territories for six years. In 1510 he took over Goa which was afterwards to become so wealthy that it was known as *Golden*; and pushing eastward he seized Malacca in the following year. This gave him control of the Straits through which the China trade flowed towards the West and from it he established links with Java, Siam, Pegu and Cochin China.

When he died in 1515 the way to Cathay was open and Portugal was paramount through all the length of it. He had colonised Goa by marrying members of his forces to the widows of Moslems killed in the fighting and respecting the customs of the country did everything he could to preserve them; but at the same time he established schools and did not hesitate to take Hindus into his employment, not as mere body-servants but as clerks in his godowns and responsible officials in his administration.

From Malacca in 1511 he sent an expedition to explore the Moluccas. It consisted of three ships under the command of Antonio de Abreu and Francisco Serrão, who pops up later in the story as a devoted friend of Magellan. After touching at Java and Amboina they pushed on, but the ships lost contact and Serrão was wrecked on an uninhabited island. He survived and made his way by native boat to Ternate where he went into the service of the Sultan. Meanwhile Abreu, prevented by head-winds from getting any farther north and east, loaded up with nutmegs and cloves at Banda and then returned to Malacca.

In 1514 a very tentative expedition was sent to China, a venture which proved to be commercially successful but achieved nothing significant politically. The Portuguese believed very strongly in the follow-through, however, and in the same year an Italian in their service named Rafael Perestrello travelled there in a junk and came back with a rich cargo and expressions of goodwill from the Chinese. He was followed in June 1517 by Fernão Peres de Andrade, an apothecary by trade and probably the first ever

19 The market-place in Goa (*c.* 1599) from an engraving by the de Bry brothers in J. H. Linschoten's *Navigatio ac itinerarium*

44

sea-borne plant-collector, who led a convoy of eight ships. The size of the expedition can be guessed by the fact that his own ship, the *Esphera*, stands in the record as being of 800 tons. It got into the Canton river and Andrade's tact and ability laid the foundations on which a close and profitable relationship with China could have been built; but his successor failed to measure up to the opportunities he had created and it was another forty years – in 1557 – before the Portuguese were able to establish their colony at Macao. During that time they were forbidden to trade with China, but it was always a gamble worth taking and in 1542 three men – Antonio da Mota, Francisco Zeimoto and Antonio Peixoto – loaded a cargo of skins in Siam and sailed for Chincheu. Their craft, which was a junk, was blown off course in a typhoon and after drifting about for some fifteen days, raised 'islands unknown to them' which turned out to be Japan.

After that a Portuguese poet said of his countrymen: '*E se mais mundo houvera, lá chegara*', which translated means 'If there had been more of the world, they would have reached it.' That ignores Australia, North America, the Pacific Islands and quite a bit more but is not really so outrageous as that kind of boasting goes. As a people they had backed the vision and forward-thinking of one man – Henry the Navigator – and though the doing of it had cost a hundred years of continuous effort and untold suffering, they had come in the end to Cathay by the Cape.

20   Map showing the ultimate extent
           of Portuguese penetration eastward
           into the Pacific Ocean

1 Lisbon	6 Mossel Bay	11 Bombay	16 Negapatam	21 Kagoshima
2 Sagres	7 Mozambique	12 Goa	17 Java	22 Kyoto
3 Cape Verde	8 Zanzibar	13 Calicut	18 Malacca	23 Tokyo
4 Walfisch Bay	9 Malindi	14 Cochin	19 Ternate	
5 Cape of Good Hope	10 Socotra	15 Ceylon	20 Canton	

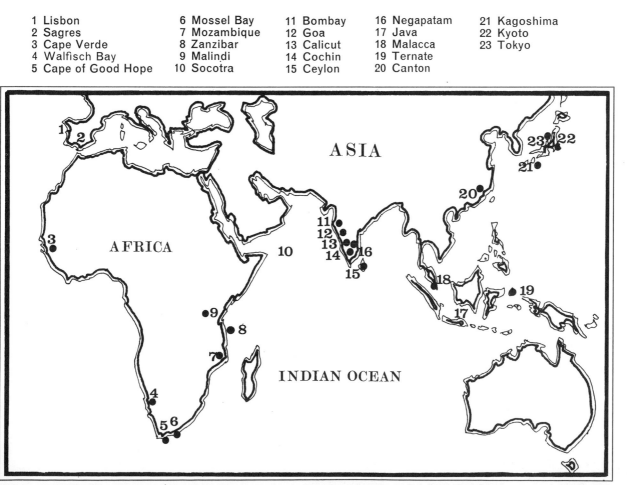

Westward to Cipangu

1 THE COSMOGRAPHER'S DREAM

ONE OF THE INESCAPABLE POLITICAL REALITIES of that era in the history of seafaring known as *the age of discovery* is the tense rivalry between the two Iberian peoples, Spain and Portugal. This has been presented in various ways, some commentators favouring one side, some the other; but economic considerations rather than religious ones or high moral principles were undeniably at the bottom of it; both sides were out to grab the plums and had no qualms about using the Christian Church and even the Pope himself as a means to that end. The Portuguese proved to be just that little bit shrewder and tougher than the Spaniards, a shade more practical maybe and clearer-sighted about their objectives. They also had a head-start thanks to the genius of the Navigator and in the short term they scooped the pool; but in the long run the voyages made in the name of Spain were probably more important in their far-reaching effects on mankind. The curious thing, however, is that with all this passionate nationalism the three men who won greatest fame in the period were neither Spanish nor Portuguese, but Italians, and all of them swopped sides without compunction.

The Portuguese were inspired by the vision of a man who never lost touch with hard reality but the Spaniards pursued a seaman's hunch backed by nothing more than a cosmographer's dream. Moreover that dream, worked up into a plan of action, had already been offered to and rejected by Portugal before Spain took it up.

The dreamer was the Florentine, Paolo dal Pozzo Toscanelli. He was the head of a family of merchant bankers and had links with the Medici. The special business concerns of his house were skins and spices and his interest in geographical discovery and trade expansion was anything but academic. Paolo was a man of many parts – doctor of medicine, astronomer, ascetic, vegetarian, mathematician, map-collector and map-maker as well as cosmographer; and of the last as already noted he has been called the greatest of his day.

In a world where trade had become the mainspring of power and the source of true greatness, the city-state of Florence ranked high. Following the capture of Constantinople by the Moslems in 1453 she had displaced Venice as the most important trading centre in the Mediterranean basin and continued to expand. Pohl in his *Pilot Major* calls her 'the Wall Street of the 15th century' and credits her with having no less than eighty banking houses through which she controlled the whole financial structure of Europe. But her merchant princes and oligarchs were also cultured men. 'No one understood so well as they that trade and learning were handmaidens' and they established the first public library in Europe as well as giving the world the lead in art and science. Leonardo da Vinci was a Florentine, so was Michelangelo, and the cultural background that threw up these great painters not only produced Toscanelli and his dream but also, as shall be seen, the practical man who set out to prove it.

For the sake of coherence and clarity it is necessary to pick up the story again in

Portugal where Prince John – King John II to be – had just accepted the responsibility for carrying on Henry the Navigator's great project. John's was an enquiring mind, healthily sceptical and taking nothing as read, not even this long-pursued objective of a sea-route to India on which so much treasure and vitality had been expended. He knew his own seafaring people were divided about it, and some among them believed that since the world was a sphere the easiest way to the Spice Islands was not the terrifyingly improbable route round the African continent but westwards across the ocean. And he had to know the hows and the whys, the pros and the cons, and weigh them for himself. Asking around for exact information he discovered that Fernão Martins, a Canon of Lisbon, had met Toscanelli and discussed the problem with him; that Toscanelli 'held the way of the West perfectly possible' and that it was 'certainly shorter and easier than the way of the East. . . .' (Madariaga, p 76). The Canon was instructed to obtain from Toscanelli a 'definite statement of his scheme'. There followed a letter from Toscanelli addressed to the Canon and dated 25 June 1474 from which Madariaga quotes as follows:

> . . . [enclosing] a map made by my own hands from which you should begin to make the journey ever towards the West and the places which you should reach and how far from the Pole or from the equinoctial line you ought to turn, and how many leagues you will have to cross to reach those regions most fertile in all kinds of spices and jewels and precious stones; and think it not marvellous that I call West the land of spices, while it is usually said that spices come from the East, for whoever navigates Westward in the lower hemisphere shall always find the said paths West and whoever travels Eastward by land in the higher hemisphere shall always find the same land East.   [p 77]

The validity of this letter and of other correspondence attributed to Toscanelli has been questioned and Madariaga lists three views: (a) all is genuine; (b) all is forgery; and (c) the letter to the Canon is genuine, those to Christopher Columbus apocryphal. He himself inclines to the third view but what concerns the seafarer is the reaction of John II rather than the argument among the historians. According to Madariaga, Toscanelli was no great shakes as a cosmographer, having taken it up 'in later life, under the pressure of financial difficulties and the zest of a possibly unscientific interest in spices in which his family had traded for long'. Prince John's seamen and nautical advisers thought much the same. It is suggested the map and the scheme boiled down into six positive statements as follows:

1. *The earth is round*, which everybody knew in those days.
2. *The known continent from Lisbon to the Indian coast, by land, i.e. eastwards, covers 230 degrees of the circumference of the earth.* This was known in Lisbon to be a mistake of the old geographer Marinus of Tyr, which had been corrected by Ptolemy. Toscanelli took no notice of Ptolemy's correction and added insult to injury by increasing Marinus's mistake (220) to 230 degrees.
3. *Therefore there remain only 130 degrees of sea to cross in order to get at the Indies by sailing dead West.* This was not true, since the previous conclusion was false. The distance in degrees was greater, though by how much, opinions varied.
4. *The length of a degree being about $62\frac{1}{2}$ miles, the total distance from coast to coast was only $62\frac{1}{2} \times 130 = 8125$ miles.* The Portuguese could afford to smile at this, because most of them held $62\frac{1}{2}$ to be far too short a figure and they inclined to think the degree was at least 70 miles long.
5. *From Cabo Verde to the Coast of Asia the distance is about one-third of the sphere*, i.e. 116 degrees.
6. *Moreover, there is Antilia on the way, between which and Cipango there are 10 'spaces'*, i.e. 50 degrees.   [Madariaga, p 77]

47

But John was a practical man and he was surrounded by hard-headed experts who kept their flat feet firmly grounded; they considered Toscanelli's plan for sailing to the East via the West, then gently but firmly put it in the 15th-century equivalent of a pigeon-hole, and continued their probing for the southern tip of Africa.

2 CHRISTOPHER COLUMBUS (*c.* 1446–1506)

Into the story at this point comes one of the best-known and most controversial characters in history whose very name is spelt in half a dozen different ways and whose origins and background are still veiled in mystery in spite of, or maybe even because of, the fact that so many researchers have pursued him and so many historians written about him. He is Christopher Columbus, also known as Cristoforo Colombo, Cristobal Colón and a few other things besides.

The legendary Columbus is a truly romantic hero, nobly born, liberally educated, elegantly and richly wed. He is presented to the world as part scientist, part man of letters, part classical scholar, an expert seaman, geographer and astronomer plus whatever else the imagination can dream of, with a kind of martyrdom thrown in. By birth he was a Genoese and his ancestry could be traced back without a break to the great days of Rome. His early life, as any true romantic's should be, was wandering and wildly adventurous. It included a sojourn at the University of Pavia, service as a sea captain with King René of Provence, and voyages to England, the Arctic, the Portuguese Atlantic islands and the Guinea coast. In the middle of all this he took time off to marry 'the daughter of an illustrious noble house' and make contact with Paolo Toscanelli, the Florentine who, as already noted, sold skins and spices for his living and made maps on the side. Through Toscanelli, he was convinced that it was possible to reach the eastern shores of Asia directly by sailing to the west. Already domiciled in Portugal he put his idea to the King who refused to back it but tried to cash in on it by sending out an expedition behind Christopher's back. As might be expected, an enterprise founded on such base treachery was a total failure and when he found out about it, Columbus shook the dust of Portugal from his sea-boots and went over to Spain where he petitioned for the support of the fair Queen Isabella. It took him seven years but in the end he got it and in 1492 sailed west, found what he thought were the

21   Christopher Columbus. Attributed to Ridolfo Ghirlandaio

48

islands lying off the eastern shore of Asia and returned to claim the fabulous rewards that had been promised to him. His success made him many enemies in high places and though he reached a position of the greatest possible honour, in the end they brought him down. He was deprived of his Governorship of the Indies and shipped home in disgrace.

> He was cast off and neglected by the monarchs he had served so well, but he carried out further explorations at his own expense and though he failed to find the Indies that he sought, he alone gave to Castile a new world. He was allowed to die forgotten in poverty and obscurity, while others reaped the rewards that were his due.

Such in bare outline (says Newton, pp 74–6) is the traditional story. It is made up almost entirely from statements of Columbus or his published writings supplemented with bits from his son Ferdinand and his friend Bishop Bartolomé de las Casas; but modern scholarship has exposed the inconsistencies in it and completely exploded it as a myth. The man is revealed as a great and incorrigible boaster, not particularly intelligent or very well educated, unscientific in both the method and content of his thinking, opinionated to the point of obsession, with a chip as big as a tree-trunk on his shoulder and a kind of perversity that would never let him give up or admit an error. Madariaga suggests he was a *converso*, a Jew accepting Christianity to escape the current persecutions, and that he could never shed the consequent guilt. These, however, are judgments, analyses, and the concern here is with the facts so far as they can be ascertained at this distance in time from contemporary writings and records.

This is an immediately more fruitful line which reveals that Colombo was a common name in northern Italy and those bearing it were not necessarily connected with the noble families that do so. In the archives of the city of Genoa a number of facts are recorded about one of the name, Domenico Colombo, who came from a family of weavers at Terra Rossa near by. In 1451 he fathered a son, his first child, who was christened Cristoforo. Some time after that the weaving trade struck a bad patch and Domenico moved with his family to Savona where he became a tavern-keeper. He seems to have been a bit feckless, however, and did a stretch in prison for debt. Nothing Cristoforo could do – and he did plenty for he was a loving son with a powerful feeling of *family* – could set him straight and he died bowed down by the weight of what he owed, in or around 1499. In the interim he had begotten two more sons and a daughter of whom only the second boy – Bartolomeo – made the history books.

Cristoforo, if the records are to be believed, was kicking around Genoa and Savona until he had passed his nineteenth birthday and whenever he pops up it is as a weaver or a wool-worker or in association with tailors or boot-makers, and never by any chance in connection with ships and seafaring men. Even when in the end he did go to sea on a voyage to the Levant it wasn't as a seaman but as a drummer or some other kind of commercial traveller; and of that voyage Newton says:

> . . . We do not know when he returned from the Levant but in 1476 he was taking part in a voyage to the West that marked the beginning of his historical career.   [p 78]

By the end of 1479 he was settled in Portugal, probably following his brother, Bartolomeo, to Lisbon and finding him already set up in the chart-making business there. This brought the two brothers into close contact with seafaring men sailing out of the port to the Atlantic Islands and in the Guinea trade. It marked the emergence of Cristoforo and was the starting-point of his rise to fame and fortune. His marriage

49

appears to be an important factor. It took place in 1480 and the bride was Felipa Moniz Perestrello whose father was the hereditary captain of the island of Porto Santo in the Madeiras. Nothing is known of the lead-up to or the circumstances surrounding this wedding but Madariaga basing himself on a contemporary writer named Oviedo says he married her out of a convent on the island and he was twenty-seven years old at the time. Oviedo, who seems to have been more than somewhat of a romanticist himself, describes the bridegroom as:

> . . . of a good size and looks, taller than the average and of sturdy limbs; the eyes lively and the other features of the face in good proportion; the hair very red; and the complexion somewhat flushed and freckled; a good speaker, cautious and of great talent and an elegant latinist and a most learned cosmographer, graceful when he wished, irate when he was crossed. [quoted Madariaga, p 83]

Subsequent exact knowledge makes this sound rather like a P.R.O. man's hand-out to the Press about a film-star; but the fact remains he was attractive enough to a young girl immured in a convent on a small island remote in the Atlantic and she threw her cap over the windmill for him.

Another writer of the period, Bartolomé de las Casas (also quoted by Madariaga), suggested that Cristoforo's main reason for marrying a Perestrello of Porto Santo was their connection 'with the foremost base of discovery at the time'.

> . . . and so he went to live in the island of Porto Santo . . . very likely owing to that only reason that he wanted to navigate, leaving there his wife, and because in that island as well as in that of Madeira, close to it, and recently discovered then, there was then beginning to be a great concourse of ships to populate and settle it, and there was frequent news every day of the fresh discoveries that were being made.
> [Las Casas, quoted by Madariaga, p 87]

The suggestion has been made that Cristoforo got his big idea from documents given to him by his mother-in-law and belonging to the Perestrellos; but this is conclusively disproved and it is virtually certain that he already knew of Toscanelli's brain-child when he went to the Madeiras. There is even a possibility that he had actually read and maybe copied the Florentine's letter to King John II. But either way, the idea had taken root in his mind and his heart and was already on the way to becoming the obsession that finally robbed him of the ultimate greatness.

Cristoforo could not accept Toscanelli's scheme as the last word but worked at it to make its basic premises tie in with other authorities he had read and, if his marginal notes are any guide, only half digested. D'Ailly, the French theologian, was one, El Fargani, an Arabian cosmographer, another and Esdras of the Apocrypha a third. His attitude, approach and method (if it can be called that) are perhaps best illustrated by a quotation from a letter he wrote to the King and Queen of Spain in 1502.

> I have said that in the carrying out of this enterprise of the Indies neither reason nor mathematics nor maps were any use to me; fully accomplished were the words of Isaiah.
> [quoted Madariaga, p 100]

Again in one of the many marginal notes he wrote in his copy of d'Ailly, he asserts:

> The earth is inhabited even to the regions in which are the cardinal extremities of the world where days last six months. There live the happiest peoples who only die of weariness of living. [quoted Madariaga, p 101]

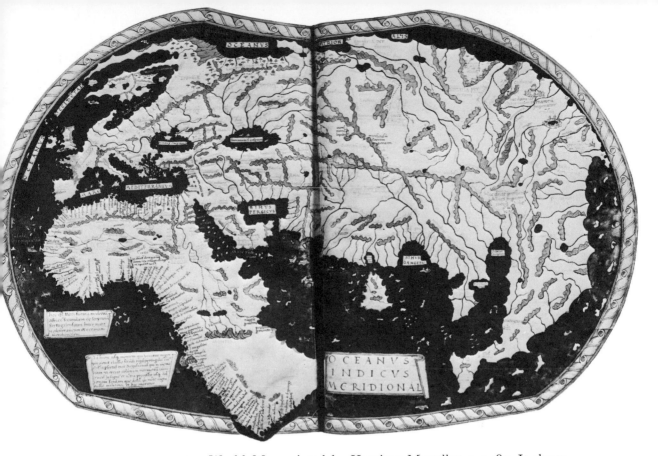

22 World Map printed by Henricus Martellus, *c.* 1489. It shows
the world as Columbus probably conceived it before he
sailed. Asia is shown according to Ptolemy and Marco
Polo, and Africa as revealed by Dias; the New World is
missing and Columbus imagined the Far East to be only
3,000 miles west of Europe

Whatever Esdras wrote or intended to convey Cristoforo took from him as gospel
that only a seventh part of the earth's surface was water. It was divided equally between
the Northern and Southern Hemispheres and from that it followed that the distance
between Spain and India by sea was only one-seventh of the earth's circumference or
51 degrees of fifty-six and two-thirds miles each.

This was his great secret, his fundamental discovery; that Cipangu and Cathay
or the islands off their eastern shores were not 8,125 watery miles away to the westward
but only 2,550. He didn't have to prove it by argument; he *knew*; he reckoned the
knowledge was worth a king's ransom; and his next step was to the King's court to
strike a bargain for it.

But discovery was the vogue. Every rogue and vagabond adventurer in western
Europe who had an idea or a dream to peddle and could raise the fare or thumb a lift
to Lisbon was there seeking a quick way to John II's ear with lavish promises; and
Cristoforo found himself only one among many. Nevertheless somehow he made it
and the proposition he put to the King is recorded in las Casas:

51

He proposed his affair to the King of Portugal, and what he offered to do was as follows: that by way of the West towards the Auster or South he would discover great lands, islands and terra firma, most happy, most rich in gold and silver and pearls and precious stones and infinite peoples; and that by that way, he intended to come upon lands of India and the great island of Cipango and the kingdoms of the Grand Khan.

[quoted Madariaga, p 111]

In return all he asked for was (1) '. . . that he should be honoured and armed a Knight with golden spurs'; (2) that he should be given the title of *Grand Admiral of the Ocean Sea* with 'all the pre-eminences and prerogatives, privileges, rights, dues and immunities enjoyed by the Admiral of Castile'; (3) that he should be 'perpetual Viceroy and governor of all the islands and terra firma which he might discover in person or which might come to be discovered through his industry'. That was only the beginning and it was when he got down to brass tacks that he really let himself go. He demanded

. . . the tenth of all the income accruing to the King from all things of gold, silver, pearls, precious stones, metals, spices and other profitable things, and from all kinds of goods bought, exchanged, found or conquered within the limits of his Admiralty. . . .

[Madariaga, p 112]

And, perhaps as a bonus, he claimed the right to a one-eighth share in the expenses and profits of any expedition to the newly discovered lands.

Barros, a contemporary Portuguese historian, describes the King's dusty answer:

The King, seeing that this Christovam Colom was a babbler and a vainglorious man in showing off his ability and more fantastic and (full of) imaginations about his island of Cypango than accurate in what he said, gave him little credit. Yet under the stress of his importunacies (the King) sent him to Dom Diogo Ortiz, Bishop of Ceuta and to Master Rodrigo and Master Josope, to whom the King usually referred these matters of cosmography and discovery and they all held as vanity the words of Christovam Colom as it was all based on imaginations and things of the Island of Cypango of Marco Polo.

[quoted Madariaga, p 113]

Cristoforo got the message and realising at last that he was flogging a dead horse in Portugal, quietly slipped his moorings and headed for Spain. His wife had died in the meantime leaving him with a five-year-old son, Diego; and the heart aches for this lonely man, so much the visionary, so much possessed by an idea, so stupidly courageous and wrong-headed in the pursuit of it, as he comes to the Spanish port of Palos near Huelva where his sea-greened statue still greets the present-day mariner pushing up the Rio Tinto out of Cadiz Bay.

There is more than one version of what happened in Palos and the chronological succession of events has never been well and truly sorted out; but the salient facts are clear enough. It was here that Cristoforo met the Pinzons. Las Casas says:

. . . amid the inhabitants (of Palos) there were three brothers of the name of Pinzon. They were rich seamen and persons of condition. One of them was called Martin Alonzo who was the richest and most considered of the three; the second was called Vicente Yanez and the third Francisco Martinez. Almost all the inhabitants of the town were under their influence for they were the richest and the best connected people there.

[quoted Newton, pp 87–8]

One account has it that Martin Alonso on a voyage to Rome with a cargo of sardines had been taken into the Pope's library and there shown a book or manuscript

52

arguing the possibility of reaching Cipangu by sailing west; and it is as near certain as makes no matter that Cristoforo entered into some kind of agreement with the Pinzons before he left to make his ultimate bid for royal patronage at the court of Isabella in Granada. In the event, the Pinzons proved indispensable to him for though he came back this time with a royal letter ordering the citizens of Palos to put two armed caravels at his disposal and covering every difficulty that might lie in the way of getting them to sea, the aforesaid citizens wanted no part of it and refused to co-operate. Obviously the Pinzons were behind this obstruction and Cristoforo was equally obviously anxious to cut them out of the enterprise. He had even gone to the extent of obtaining royal permission to recruit his crews from the local prison with the promise of free pardon for those who would chance their arm. But Martin Alonso had the edge and in the end it was he who sorted out the ships, provisioned and equipped them and recruited the crews to man them.

Witnesses in a subsequent lawsuit between the parties testified to his diligence and drive, declaring:

> To some he said they would be raised above their poverty; to others that they would find there houses with tiles of gold; to some he offered good fortune, and for every man he had pleasant words and money; so that with this and the general trust in him, many people followed him from the towns.   [quoted Madariaga, p 192]

Another claimed he said:

> Friends, come away, come away with us; you are all here crawling in misery; come away on this voyage, for, according to fame, we shall find gold-roofed houses and you shall all come back rich and happy.   [quoted Madariaga, p 192]

And the old lure worked its magic again. Columbus got his crews and his ships – three instead of two in the end. They were *La Pinta*, commanded by Martin Alonso Pinzon, *La Niña*, under Vicente Yanez Pinzon, and the *Marigalante*, owned and captained by the celebrated pilot Juan de la Cosa. She at about 220 tons (one version gives her a precise 233), was the biggest of the three, with castles both fore and aft and square-rigged. Her length is given as 117 feet, that of the *Pinta* as 51 feet with the *Niña* shorter than that again, and lateen-rigged.

Madariaga says the ships were named by 'amorous seamen', that *La Pinta* meant 'the Painted One'; *La Niña*, 'the Girl'; and worst of all, *Marigalante*, 'frivolous Mary'. The last one in particular was an offence to Columbus and he immediately had it changed to *Santa Maria*.

Accounts about the total number of people in the three ships vary but Newton puts it at 'from 90 to 120' and Madariaga is more precise. He says, quoting las Casas, there were ninety seamen plus another twenty or thirty persons including '. . . several officers of the King who fancied to sail with him out of curiosity, as well as domestic servants and acquaintances of his' (p 192). There were no women which is not surprising and no priests which is. On provisions we have the word of Diego de Valera (also quoted by Madariaga) that the recognised and expected allowance for each man was one pound of biscuits, slightly over two litres of wine and two-thirds of a pound of meat or fish per day, plus such items as cheese, onions and other vegetables (probably peas and beans) and oil and vinegar presumably *ad lib*. The ships were ballasted with ammunition for the artillery and in addition carried a small cargo of 'glass beads,

23 Columbus takes possession of Hispaniola. An etching by Theodore de Bry dated 1594. It combines two separate incidents. On the left the explorer lands on the island of Guanahani. He erects cross and dedicates island to Our Lord (San Salvador). Columbus carries royal spear ashore – to show he was intent on the spread of Christianity and the rule of Spain. On the right he meets the people of Hispaniola (Haiti) on 6 December 1492. From *Americae pars quarta* (Frankfurt, 1594)

mirrors, coloured bonnets, pins and needles to charm into Christian ways the simple heathens whom he expected to discover' (Madariaga, p 195).

The total investment represented by the expedition is estimated by Madariaga to have been 2,040,000 *maravedis*, made up as follows:

	Maravedis
Hire of caravels, 500 tons at 2,000 *maravedis* per ton	1,000,000
Upkeep for one year	540,000
Other expenses	500,000

Of this not inconsiderable sum a million *maravedis* was supplied by the crown and half a million put up by Columbus himself after he had borrowed it from Martin Alonso. That left half a million to account for, most if not all of which was presumably put in by the Pinzon family.

Columbus sailed from Palos on his momentous voyage on 3 August 1492, heading for the Canaries where he had some kind of trouble with the *Pinta*, caused he believed by some of her crew getting cold feet about pushing off into the unknown. This in spite of a royal promise of a life pension of 10,000 *maravedis* for the first man to sight land. Nevertheless he got away from Gomera on 6 September, steering as near as he could make it due west along the 28th parallel.

Much has been made of the difficulties encountered on the voyage, the doubts and fears of the crews, the unflagging energy and unwavering faith with which Columbus kept them going and so on; but apart from some bewilderment due to magnetic variation, the voyage, at least according to Newton, '. . . was in reality a prosperous and uneventful' one. Land was raised at two o'clock in the morning of 12 October, that is thirty-six days out from Gomera which, taking everything into consideration, was pretty good going for those days.

The landfall turned out to be a small island in the group now called the Bahamas.

Its modern name is Guanahani or Watling Island but Columbus called it San Salvador and annexed it to Spain.

After two days, he pushed on into a regular maze of islands which hardened his conviction that he was off the coast of Asia and within striking distance of Cipangu. He even wrote down in his Journal that 'he believed these islands to be the innumerable ones which are set down in the maps at the end of the Orient' (Madariaga, p 214), and having seen gold ornaments worn by the inhabitants, it was gold that now possessed his passionate mind. Gold, he declared, 'is born in this island, though owing to lack of time I could not fully prove it'; and again, this time from las Casas

> The Admiral argued from this heat of which he then suffered that in these Indies and in that region where he was, there must be gold. . . . And the Admiral believed that he was near the source and that our Lord would show him where gold is born.
>
> [quoted Madariaga, pp 215–16]

His first really big discovery was Cuba which he promptly declared to be Cipangu and then decided could not possibly be because it did not tally with the descriptions given by Marco Polo. On he went again and on 5 December discovered a huge island which he annexed and named Española (Hispaniola), and this time he declared they had found the real Cipangu and stuck to it. Moreover he was convinced that what they had seen of Cuba could only be part of the Asiatic continent. Commenting on this Newton says:

> . . . It seems extraordinary that one who had set out to find islands in the Atlantic should not have realised that he had discovered new lands and should have deluded himself into the error of believing that what he had found was but the extremity of the ancient world. Columbus was . . . a visionary and a mystic who having once formed a belief held to it with extraordinary mental obstinacy and persistently sought in his pseudo-scientific knowledge of medieval geography and the Scriptures for reasons to support the delusion . . . having once adopted it, he maintained it to the very day of his death. [pp 92–3]

Meanwhile Martin Alonso Pinzon in the *Pinta* had fallen out with Columbus over a number of things and, taking advantage of his ship's superior sailing qualities, he now went off on his own. What was in his mind is anybody's guess. Some say his departure was involuntary, others that he had taken all he could stomach of the Admiral's arrogance and big-headed egotism, others again that he had conceived the idea of reaching back to Castile ahead of Columbus to grab off the honour and glory accruing for the voyage. What he in fact did, was to go to Española (which incidentally he too thought was Cipangu) where he acquired by barter a considerable quantity of gold.

Gold was the lure and though he was tormented now with fears of Martin Alonso getting home before him to steal his thunder, Columbus continued to cruise around in quest of it. He also did a spot of surveying and the record says 'he left no bay unexplored, no hill uncharted, no bottom unsounded'; but his luck was running out again and at midnight on Christmas Day 1492 the *Santa Maria* piled herself up on a hidden reef and became a total loss.

His response to this disaster reveals the complexity of his character, that strange mixture in him of the visionary and the man of action, the religious mystic and the practical man of the sea. He saw himself as a man of destiny; therefore there was no room in his life for blind chance and it followed that the wreck was God's will. It had

55

to be; and his first concern was to discover God's purpose in willing it. Looking around him and counting heads, he realised he now had two crews and only one ship and she was much too small to carry them all home. Then he understood, and from that moment it was obvious to him that God's purpose was that he, Christopher Columbus, should leave a settlement on this fabulous island of Cipangu which he had discovered. And with all the energy and organising skill of a true seafarer he set about it.

First he built a fort which he armed and stored with ample ammunition and provisions for a year; then he named it *Villa de la Navidad*, appointed Diego de Arana and Pedro Gutiérrez as joint commanders and picked out thirty-eight men to stay behind under their orders. Navarrete (an authority much quoted by Madariaga) says at this point:

> He concluded that Cipango was in that island (i.e. Espanola) and that there is in it abundance of gold, spices, musk and rhubarb. [quoted Madariaga, p 226]

and hugging this to him while he sweated blood about Martin Alonso and the whole tribe of Pinzons, he tripped his anchor and made sail aboard the *Niña* for home on 4 January 1493.

On the second day out he met with the missing *Pinta* and had her master up on the carpet. There was a flaming row but no blood was shed and nobody was hanged, a fact to be remembered later when characters like Magellan and Drake begin to strut across the stage. His failure to punish Martin Alonso for the desertion is taken by some commentators as indicative of the Admiral's inability to stand up to strong personalities; but it must not be forgotten that Martin Alonso was only one of the Pinzons and Columbus was surrounded by and to a considerable extent in the power of the others.

The passage home was both longer and more difficult than the voyage out. Columbus made a more northerly course, but between his need to maintain the morale of his seamen and his desire to keep them in ignorance of the true location of his discoveries, he managed to create a great deal of confusion. Las Casas, transcribing his Journal, writes:

> He says that he feigned to have covered more distance in order to put the pilots and sailors who handled the charts off the track, so that he should remain the sole lord of the road to the Indies, as indeed he remains, for not one of them had noted down the way aright, so that no one can be sure of his way to the Indies. [quoted Madariaga, p 233]

Caught up as he was in such a web of deception behind such a veil of secrecy, the wonder is that he ever made another landfall. But he did, at Santa Maria, the southernmost island of the Azores, on 18 February. After some unpleasantness with the Portuguese Captain of the Port, he got away from there on the 24th. The weather was bad but the wind westerly and he ran before it with bare poles and all the time his heart in his mouth for dread of the disaster that seemed inevitable. Again the ships parted company. Then on 4 March Columbus raised the land in the vicinity of the mouth of the Tagus and although this meant putting himself at the mercy of the Portuguese again, he ran into the river and anchored.

Columbus stayed in Lisbon just over a week and if people like Barros are to be believed, far from keeping quiet about his voyage and his discoveries, he broadcast them, blown up and trimmed to suit the occasion, till even the King got the message and summoned him to an audience. Some historians would have it he was lucky ever

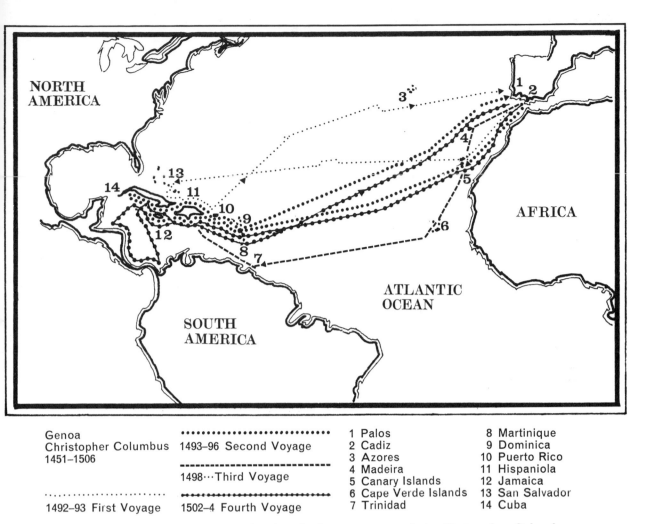

Genoa	••••••••••••••••••••	1 Palos
Christopher Columbus	1493–96 Second Voyage	2 Cadiz
1451–1506		3 Azores
	- - - - - - - - - - - - - - - - - -	4 Madeira
	1498···Third Voyage	5 Canary Islands
····················	•-•-•-•-•-•-•-•-•-•-•-•	6 Cape Verde Islands
1492–93 First Voyage	1502–4 Fourth Voyage	7 Trinidad

8 Martinique	
9 Dominica	
10 Puerto Rico	
11 Hispaniola	
12 Jamaica	
13 San Salvador	
14 Cuba	

24   Map showing the four voyages made by Christopher Columbus

to get out of that one alive; but it would seem the net result was that King John compared the achievements of Columbus with those of Bartolomeo Dias down the Guinea coast and round into the Indian Ocean, and took a poor view of them. Deciding he was still on the best bet, he treated the boasting Admiral with ironic honour and bid him a courteous farewell.

He sailed from the Tagus on the 13th and two days later entered the harbour of Palos just over seven months after he had left it. Later on the same day Martin Alonso Pinzon, who had been sheltering up the coast near Vigo, brought in the *Pinta* and the earth-shaking, world-shaping voyage of one Genoese dreamer was over.

The concern here is with Columbus as a seafarer; consequently detailed analysis of the political, social and economic effects of his discoveries must be sought elsewhere. Two things need, however, to be noted – the immediate impact on the Caribs and the effect on the rivalry between Spain and Portugal.

That first voyage was the peak. Columbus made a second, sailing in September

1493 with seventeen ships and around 1,500 colonists. By this time he had talked so long and so loudly about the wonders and wealth of Cipangu that there was keen competition for berths and 100 men who couldn't make it legitimately stowed away in the caravels. There were no visionaries among this enormous crowd. By and large they were either layabouts looking for a soft option or greedy adventurers out for a quick profit; and the tragedy is that they seem to have brought Columbus down to somewhere near their own level.

They found the settlement of Villa de la Navidad on Española wrecked and its people either killed or scattered as a consequence of their own lust and greed towards the natives. The newcomers, however, ignored the obvious lesson and conscripted the Caribs to work in the gold-mines. Some rebelled and were forcibly loaded into five of the ships which took them to Spain where in the summer of 1495 they were sold off as slaves. Then, says J. Holland Rose:

> . . . the seizure of West African negroes was the next step downwards; and thus began an evil destined . . . not to be stayed until 1865 . . . (and) the only valuable gift of Columbus to the new lands was the introduction of the sugar cane from the Canaries and even this accentuated the demand for negro slaves. . . . [p 93]

According to Pohl the Indians shipped to Spain were the lucky ones:

> . . . Under the cruel hands of the fiendish and bloody-minded Spaniards, thousands of Indians among the islands had already suffered extermination, by direct slaughter and by the conditions of living forced upon them. The native population of San Juan Bautista (Puerto Rico) was on its way to practically total extermination. Nine tenths of the natives in Espanola perished within ten years. . . . [p 74]

So much for the blessings of civilisation! The political repercussions of the first voyage were as far-reaching in a different way. Spain and Portugal had already carved up the world outside Europe between them and under the Treaty of Toledo made in 1480 and a papal bull of the following year it had been agreed that Portugal was to have the Canaries and all lands south of them to the Indies 'beyond, behind and across the Ganges'. The discoveries of Columbus, still only vaguely and mostly erroneously interpreted, seemed to make hay of the agreement and Portugal protested loudly and long. On 4 May 1493 in an effort to stop the two countries tearing each other to pieces, the Pope issued a bull dividing 'the unknown regions of the world in half': everything east of a meridian line 100 leagues west of the Azores or the Cape Verde Islands was to be Portuguese and everything west of that line Spanish. Portugal was still unsatisfied, however, and in the new agreement finally reached on 7 June 1494 the dividing line on her insistence was drawn 370 leagues west of the Cape Verdes. The agreement became known as the Treaty of Tordesillas and its very great importance will emerge.

On this second voyage the Admiral discovered Dominica, Guadeloupe, Martinique, the Virgin Islands and Puerto Rico; and in the course of a search along the south coast of Cuba (which he still believed to be the mainland of Asia) he also located Jamaica; but in the end 'he returned to Spain in March 1496 with little to show for his efforts' (Newton, p 104).

With the luck running out on him fast, he had another try in 1498, going this time via the Cape Verde Islands and making his ultimate landfall at Trinidad from which island he went on to the coast of Venezuela. He seems to have realised this was part of a great continent, but says Newton:

. . . he was hopelessly involved in his interpretation of the discovery and his mystical imaginings and wild theories destroyed any possibility that the discovery might restore his credit at Court . . . [p 111]

This venture ended in him being made a prisoner by the Governor of Española and sent home in chains. He arrived in November 1500 and though he was immediately released by order of the Sovereigns, 'they never again gave him any responsibility'. Nevertheless he made one more voyage, this time financing it himself and leaving Cadiz with three caravels on 11 April 1502. He got neither welcome nor co-operation from the Spaniards now established in the Caribbean islands and squeezing them for all they would yield; but driven by that perverse, passionate and obstinate nature of his, he penetrated the Gulf to the coast of Honduras and followed the coastline south to the Isthmus of Panama.

. . . He believed he was now only 19 days sail from the mouth of the Ganges but he could find no strait through the land and he does not seem to have realised how narrow was the isthmus at this point. [Newton, p 114]

There is no doubt,. however, that his failure was aggravated by the conflict in him between his visions and the lure of gold. Always he seems to have been divided and confused not only in his thinking but also in his actions by the idea of a mountain of gold and the urgent need to find it.

He reached back to Spain, broken in health and spirit, in November 1504 and never left it again. Two years later he was dead in Valladolid and his passing caused no comment that has survived.

Misguided and self-deluded Columbus undoubtedly was, but whatever drove him and whatever his limitations, he was the forerunner and every man after him to the westward was treading to some degree in his footsteps, sailing in the wake he left. Madariaga equates him with Don Quixote and it is easy to see him as part clown, part tragedian; but however much he suffered and agonised personally – and it was plenty – his real tragedy was that of *everyman*; at the end of the day he had to be superseded by others, who, starting where he left off and learning from his mistakes, went farther than he did.

3 AMERIGO VESPUCCI (1451–1512)

An even more controversial character than Columbus, if that seems possible, was the Florentine, Amerigo Vespucci; and on balance, more dirt has been flung on his illustrious name than on that of the passionate Genoese. He has been denounced as 'a boaster, a fame-grabber who never commanded a ship, and a mounte-bank who preferred self-contradictions to truth'; he has also been described as 'an obscure ship-chandler' and Ralph Waldo Emerson wrote of him:

Strange that broad America must wear the name of a thief! Amerigo Vespucci, the pickle-dealer at Seville, who went out in 1499, a subaltern with Hojeda, and whose highest naval rank was boatswain's mate, in an expedition that never sailed, managed in this lying world to supplant Columbus and baptize half the earth with his own dishonest name! [from *English Traits*, quoted by Pohl in his foreword]

59

At the other extreme, Pohl claims 'he had all the qualifications for a ship's commanding officer' and among them lists his robust constitution, his proven ability in international trade and in managing the shore end of shipping, his skill as a cartographer, cosmographer, mathematician and astronomer, his familiarity with the contemporary aids to navigation and his intelligent, open and enquiring mind. Moreover he had friends in high places and the right kind of contacts elsewhere, and with him, unlike Columbus, obtaining financial and political backing was no problem; he had only to ask to be given.

As to the record which some would maintain is all that really counts, he was a whole year ahead of Columbus on the coast of South America and the first ever from the Old World to chart the coastline of Central America, Mexico and the southeastern coast of the United States.

Vespucci was born in Florence in 1451, and belonged to a family reputed to be connected in some way with Spanish Royalty but which was in fact engaged in trade. They must have had some kind of political pull for in 1478 Amerigo was in the diplomatic service and spent the next two years in France as private secretary to the ambassador. It was here he learned his way about among worldly ambitious men and the experience paid off handsomely in later life. After returning from France he put three years into the family business, then in 1483 was made *maestro di casa* or manager of a firm belonging to the Medici. It was a position of great trust and presumably of equally great opportunity. The firm was in the overseas trade and:

> . . . dealt in fish, wine, cherries, buttermilk, curds, mustard, cloth, shirts, handkerchiefs, sheets, towels, bed curtains, mulberry seed, tapestry, carpets, tablecloths, napkins, silver forks, spoons, knives, saltcellars, satchels, poultry, pigeons, goblets . . . and so forth.
>
> [Pohl, p 28]

On the side, he collected books about cosmography and astronomy and maps, especially maps. One of his treasures was a portolano on sheepskin, made in Mallorca by Gabriel de Velasca and dated 1439. For this he paid 130 ducats which Pohl reckons to be 400 dollars in modern currency. This gives some indication of his passionate interest in things connected with ships and seafaring.

In 1492 he was in Barcelona chasing up a cargo of salt and at the end of that year set up house in Seville where, starting as the agent of the Medici, he eventually became

25   Amerigo Vespucci. A Florentine portrait

the leading outfitter of ships, a kind of super ship-chandler. As such he must have mixed a great deal with seafaring people and there is no doubt at all that he knew about the voyage of Bartolomeo Dias round the Cape of Good Hope which had been made five years before. Presumably he also knew that a crazy Genoese called Columbus had sailed from Palos the previous summer, heading west to find the East.

He was there in Seville when Columbus returned proclaiming loudly and with trimmings that he had discovered 'the islands beyond the Ganges . . . and reached the mainland of Asia'. He was still there when the Genoese returned to a distinctly cool reception from his second voyage, and it was during the third one that Vespucci reached the conclusion that Columbus had failed and decided to find the western route to Asia himself. Word had come that Vasco da Gama had reached India sailing eastwards via the Cape; this for Portugal. He, Amerigo Vespucci, would sail westwards for Spain and finding a way through the islands already discovered, or round them, come to Cape Catigara and the narrow strait which Marco Polo had described as the sea-route from Cathay and Java and the Spice Islands into the Great Sinus and the incalculable wealth and trade of India.

He too was basing himself on Ptolemy as modified by Toscanelli with whom he had contact through an uncle in the Church.

Vespucci asked and was given the green light and all he needed. His first expedition sailed from Cadiz on 18 May 1499. It consisted of four (though some records say six) ships under what Pohl claims was the nominal command of a young courtier named Alonso de Hojeda who had been a junior officer on the second voyage of Columbus. Another shipmate of the Genoese went with Vespucci as 'one of the pilots'. He was that Juan de la Cosa who had owned, commanded and lost the *Santa Maria* in Cristoforo's first voyage and then captained the *Niña* on his second venture. Vespucci's position seems to have been more than slightly ambiguous. Pohl says he went in a 'two-fold capacity' – as 'an astronomer or one who knew cosmography and matters pertaining to the sea . . . and also as a merchant' (Herrera, quoted by Pohl, p 49). *Por mercader* was the precise term and it is interpreted as meaning he was the representative of the financial backers and there to see their interests, policies and purposes were pursued. From that angle his main task was to see they got their money's worth in new commercial opportunities and markets. Pohl adds:

> He was not compelled to take orders from Hojeda . . . the expedition was a commercial venture and was expected to pay for itself. . . . Amerigo's backers must have insisted that the route to be followed by the sailing masters conform to the promising plan expressed by Amerigo: 'It was my intention to see whether I could turn a headland that Ptolemy calls the Cape of Catigara which connects with the Sinus Magnus.' [pp 49–50]

There is an illustration of two of Vespucci's ships on a map drawn by Juan de la Cosa in 1500. They were three-masters with the main very much taller than the fore and mizzen; and though Pohl refers to them as caravels they were more truly square-rigged ships for they were lateen-rigged only on the mizzen. Forward they had a steep-tilted bowsprit carrying a small square sail used to improve the steering running before the wind and on the mainmast of one was a circular platform or castle possibly designed as a vantage point for the look-out man.

The hazards of the Atlantic crossing had by this time become fairly well known. It was still a bit of a gamble but nothing like so crazy as when Columbus made his bid.

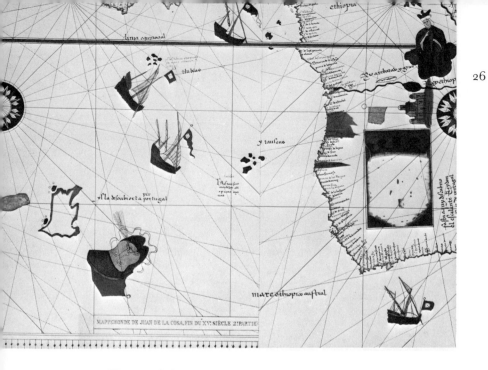

26 Vespucci's ships as drawn on the map of Juan de la Cosa dated 1500

Vespucci (or Hojeda, whichever is preferred) had fair winds all the way and, sailing 3,700 miles in twenty-four days, made a landfall about 5 degrees south of that made by Columbus on his third voyage, i.e. either in Surinam or French Guiana. This represents an average speed throughout of 6·5 knots which is fantastic for the time and better going than many an early 20th-century tramp steamer made in the River Plate grain trade. Having reached the coast, the expedition now split up and while one part under Hojeda turned north avid for treasure, the other, under Vespucci, turned south in search of Cathay.

On 27 June, Vespucci sighted land again 4 degrees north of the Equator and Pohl claims this was the first sight of Brazil.

> ... Amerigo's landfall in Brazil preceded that of Vicente Yanez Pinzon by seven months, that of Diego de Lepe by eight months and that of Pedro Alvares Cabral by ten months....
>
> [p 52]

Coasting southward they turned into a huge gulf which was named by Vespucci *Gulf of Santa Maria* and turned out to be the mouth of the Amazon. The vegetation – mostly mangroves – was, it is reported, so dense it was impossible to land and pushing on they found the Pará river, and sailed up it for 100 miles. Altogether about twelve days were spent in this area, but Cape Catigara beckoned and presently they drove on, sailing south and east between 700 and 800 miles in ten days. By this time, 24 July, Vespucci had encountered the adverse South Equatorial Current which slowed him down and in the end forced him to give up hope of further progress. Reluctantly he got his ships around and headed back to the north-west.

This decision must have cost him an enormous effort to make. According to his reckoning the entrance to the Great Sinus lay in about $8\frac{1}{2}$ degrees south and there he was already in 6 to $6\frac{1}{2}$ south. In point of fact he overestimated his southing and was 2 degrees out in his calculations. Still, 2 degrees of latitude is nothing much on the scale in which he was dreaming and putting his ships about would just tear him apart.

Following the coast northward, he came without much excitement to Trinidad and the Gulf of Paria where he was tempted to stay and collect pearls; but he was still hoping to find that elusive passage to India and thinking the coast of Venezuela was the mainland of Asia, he went on steadily groping along it till he got to the region of La Guaira where he ran into trouble with the natives. Some of his men received arrow wounds and to teach the Indians a lesson Amerigo massacred 150 of them and burned 180 of their houses, which, he being a Florentine, proves among other things that bloody-mindedness was not the monopoly of the Spaniard.

The battle, if it can be so designated, forced the expedition to stop over for twenty days for the wounded to recuperate and this period – from about 17 August till 5 September – was marked, according to Pohl, by Vespucci's greatest achievement in navigation. Laid up there under the towering mountains that guarded the interior from the sea, he '. . . evolved a valid astronomical method of determining longitude' (p 62).

Previous to this, as already noted, longitude was a matter of dead-reckoning, a kind of inspired guesswork based on the sand-glass for time and the log-line for speed. 'Amerigo Vespucci,' Pohl continues, 'brought a fresh mind to the problem . . . and was the first man to place it on a scientific basis. . . .' Determining longitude on board a ship at sea to be used as a continuous guide in navigation was still a very long way off. It waited, as Pohl points out, on really accurate tables for the movement of celestial bodies, and on the development of precise measuring instruments including a clock that would keep exact time in a moving ship; but Vespucci was involved in a more urgent problem, that outlined by Ptolemy centuries before:

'The correct course would be for any person attempting to draw a map of the world, to lay down as the basis of it those points that were determined by the most correct observations, and to fit into it those derived from other sources, so that their positions may suit as well as possible with the principal points thus laid down in the first instance.' The task

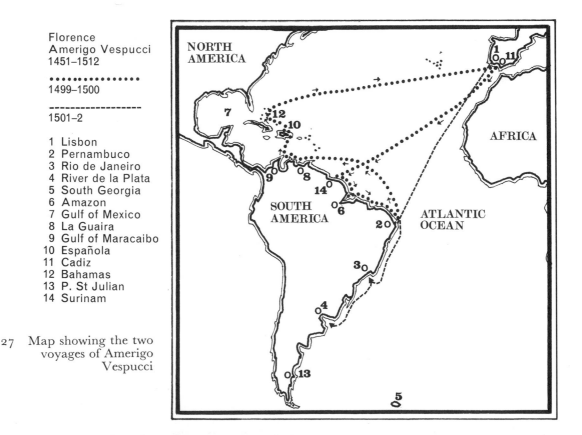

Florence
Amerigo Vespucci
1451–1512

•••••••••••••
1499–1500

- - - - - - - - - - -
1501–2

1 Lisbon
2 Pernambuco
3 Rio de Janeiro
4 River de la Plata
5 South Georgia
6 Amazon
7 Gulf of Mexico
8 La Guaira
9 Gulf of Maracaibo
10 Española
11 Cadiz
12 Bahamas
13 P. St Julian
14 Surinam

27 Map showing the two
    voyages of Amerigo
    Vespucci

was to be accomplished from various stations on land and was to fix the meridians of the principal capes, ports, islands, and so forth throughout the world and thus lay the foundation for accurate geographical knowledge. This work Amerigo commenced on the night of the 23rd of August 1499. [p 62]

That night Vespucci observed a conjunction of the moon with Mars and from it, using a set of tables called Regiomontano's *Ephemerides astronomicae*, calculated his longitude; and Pohl claims that *after making allowance for errors in the tables*

> ... it is reasonable to say that the distances in longitude between a given port in Europe and various stations in the lands to the west of the Atlantic could be determined reliably within approx. two degrees. . . . [p 68]

Professor Taylor in *The Haven-finding Art* is rather less enthusiastic, and says:

> Columbus had thought that he found his longitude by noting an eclipse of the Moon of which the time had been foretold in Regiomontanus' *Ephemerides*, and Amerigo Vespucci had attempted a lunar distance. But the results they obtained were quite worthless – worthless that is to say as determinations of longitude, but worthwhile as pointing the need for instruments of precision to bridge the gap between theory and practice. [p 189]

Nevertheless the fundamental principle of Amerigo's method continued to be used even after the chronometer came into general use and Captain Cook is quoted as saying:

> The method of lunar distance from the sun or stars is the most priceless discovery which the navigator ever could have made and must render the memory of the first discoverer of this method immortal. [quoted Pohl, pp 68–9]

After this little interlude, the expedition pushed on along the coast of Venezuela as far as the Gulf of Maracaibo. For some time before this the ships had been leaking badly, their timbers having been attacked by the teredo worm, and now it was all the crews could do to keep them afloat. Moreover the men were in a low state, both in morale and physique, and food was running short. In these circumstances it was decided to call it a day and head for Española where they arrived after seven days sailing.

With the crews rested and refreshed and their stores replenished Amerigo and his companions left Española at the end of November and spent practically the whole winter among the reefs, shoals and sandbanks of the Bahamas; and then, 'after nearly a year at sea', the urge among the foremast hands to get homeward bound became too insistent to be ignored. The ships, however, in spite of all they had seen and the wonders they had discovered, were still empty of cargo and treasure, and it was imperative that the voyage should clear its cost and show a profit big enough for them to share in as well as the backers. A conference was held and the decision made to fill the holds with slaves who having no prime cost would be all profit in Spain. 'And so they went to certain islands and seized over 200 natives' (Pohl, p 74).

The passage home took sixty-seven days and the mind recoils from any speculation about the suffering of the 200 involuntary passengers. It is impossible to imagine their fears and mental agony and their physical condition, the degradation and loss of human dignity to which they were subjected are inconceivable to us, or were until Belsen and Auschwitz. Amerigo arrived back in Cadiz about the middle of June.

He was still determined to find Cape Catigara and the strait leading into the Great

64

Sinus, and for his second voyage he changed flags, believing that what he sought lay on the Portuguese side of the line of demarcation laid down by the Treaty of Tordesillas. It is even said he turned down an offer of three ships from the King of Spain in order to make the trip for Portugal which country was now firmly in control of the eastern route to India and rapidly building up its corner of the spice trade.

King John provided him with three ships and in Amerigo's own words quoted by Pohl, the voyage was 'solely to make discoveries, with a commission to that effect and not to seek for any profit' (p 102). Yet the venture was at least partly backed by Bartolomeo Marchioni, a Florentine who was the leading banker in Lisbon. He had a finger and a stake in all the Portuguese voyages and 'owned at least one ship in every fleet that was sent to India'.

In the meantime Vespucci's astronomical observations and the work he had put in on them were leading him to some fundamental conclusions about the circumference of the earth. Columbus made it 20,400 Roman miles as against Ptolemy's 22,500. Toscanelli had a different view and so did Eratosthenes in his day. Amerigo proved them all wrong. First, he stabilised the *league* as being $4\frac{1}{2}$ Roman miles, then worked out there were $16\frac{2}{3}$ leagues to the degree. This made a degree of longitude on the Equator 75 Roman miles and the circumference of the world round its middle 27,000 Roman miles.

> His 27,000 Roman miles at 1,620 English yards to the mile were 24,852 English miles – only 50 English miles less than the actual circumference which is 24,902 English miles. The accuracy of his estimate is so obvious, it is astonishing that it has never before been pointed out.
>
> [Pohl, p 105]

Vespucci sailed from Lisbon on his voyage for Portugal on 13 May 1501. He headed south past the Canaries to Cape Verde where he encountered two ships of Cabral's expedition returning from India, and marvelled at the richness of their cargoes:

> That which the said ships carry, coming loaded, is a great quantity of cinnamon, fresh and dried ginger, much pepper, cloves, nutmegs, mace, musk, agallochum, stomax, delicacies, porcelains, cassia, mastic, incense, myrrh, red and white sandalwood, wood aloes, camphor, amber, canes, much lacquer, mummy wax, indigo and tutty, opium, hepatic aloes, India paper and a great variety of drugs, which would be too lengthy a matter to relate. Of jewels I do not know the rest, except that I saw many diamonds, rubies and pearls, among which I saw one ruby in a round piece of most beautiful color, that weighed seven and a half carats. . . .
>
> [Letters to Lorenzo Medici, quoted by Pohl, p 129]

Leaving Cabral's fantastic argosy to battle on to the northward, Vespucci headed for the Brazilian coast and after making his landfall is reputed to have explored southward as far as San Julián (Port St Julian) which is in latitude 49·21 S. Turning northward again, he recrossed the Equator about 27 May 1502 and arrived back in Lisbon in June of the same year.

He had failed to discover Cape Catigara but he drew the correct conclusions from what he had seen and 'made his announcement of the greatest geographical fact ever revealed by any one man – a new continent', no less:

> There is much more to this earth than Europe and Asia and Africa. There is also a New

World, a new half of the earth, a never-before-dreamed-of western Hemisphere. There is a whole new continent waiting for the men of Europe to explore and possess and thereon to begin a new civilisation. . . . [Pohl, p 139]

That was the end of Vespucci's seafaring but unlike Columbus he gave up while the going was still good and his reputation in influential circles at its highest. Returning to Spain he was made *Pilot Major* of that country, an office especially created to honour him and use his peculiar talents. His job was:

. . . to examine, classify and prepare all the pilots of Spain; to teach them Piloting, navigation and cosmography; to direct the construction of hydrographic charts; to correct these and keep them up to date; to inspect and to calibrate navigational instruments; to exercise control over the important problems of overseas navigation. . . . [Pohl, p 184]

As might be imagined this kind of brief did not endear him to the old salts and tarpaulins who now came willy-nilly under his jurisdiction. In particular his attempts to teach them his method of determining longitude by lunar distance were never successful. The pilots and ship-masters argued that if Vespucci had his way their specialised knowledge and experience, their flair for dead-reckoning based on the weather and the sailing qualities of their ships would no longer be required and they would be out of a job. Consequently twelve years after his appointment a commentator, Antonio Pigafetta in *Treatise on Navigation*, could still write:

At the present time the pilots content themselves with knowing the latitude, and are so proud they will not hear speak of longitude. [quoted Pohl, p 190]

which shows how perverse a seafaring man can be when he sticks his toes in.

Vespucci died in Seville on 22 February 1512 aged fifty-eight and it is said he was quite poor. His famous captain, Juan de la Cosa, crossed the Atlantic thirteen times in all and was killed by the Indians in Venezuela two years before.

Pohl credits Vespucci with a long succession of important *firsts* which might be conveniently listed as follows:

28 Lisbon Harbour in the early 16th century. From de Bry's *America*

He was

first on the coast of Brazil;
first to explore the whole coastline of that country;
first on the coasts of Colombia, Uruguay and Argentina;
first in the rivers Amazon, Pará and del Plata;
first on an estimated total of more than 6,000 miles of hitherto unknown coastline;
first to record the Equatorial Current;
first to go south of the Equator on the western side of the Atlantic;
first to go south of the latitude by which the Portuguese rounded the Cape of Good Hope,
i.e. first to sail between the latitudes of 35 and 50 degrees south;
first to apply astronomy to the determination of longitude;
first to realise that the land he, with Columbus and a few others, had discovered was not
part of Asia but a new continent.

Finally, 'he left as a heritage to Spain and Magellan the dream of finding a passage at the southern end of America. . . .' [Pohl, p 198].

4 FERNÃO DE MAGALHÃES (1480–1521)

Once the physical reality of the New World had been accepted and acknowledged the problem of getting round or through it to China became the main preoccupation of the Spanish navigators; at first there appeared to be three possibilities – a passage to the north-west, a narrow strait through tropical Central America and a similar channel through or round the southern tip of the continent. Then the famous march of Vasco Nuñez de Balboa across the Isthmus of Darien in 1513, established the Pacific Ocean as another inescapable fact and, ruling out the middle course, cleared the way for Fernão de Magalhães whose name is better known in its anglicised form of Ferdinand Magellan.

Magellan was Portuguese and born in that country in or around 1480. At the age of twenty-five he was serving with d'Almeida in India, sailing there round the Cape in 1505. This particular tour of duty lasted seven years during which time he saw the taking of Malacca by Lopes de Sequeira and the second taking of Goa under Albuquerque in 1510. In 1512 while serving in Morocco he 'fell foul of the authorities' and made this the excuse and justification for renouncing his allegiance to Portugal and going over to Spain. This switching of flags seems to have been a popular exercise in the age of discovery and shows how lightly the seafarer wore his nationality. In Magellan's case the change-over was a matter of expediency coldly calculated. According to Newton, he had worked out that the Moluccas were just inside the sphere allotted to Spain under the Treaty of Tordesillas and:

. . . he had heard of lands lying farther to the east – Borneo, the Philippines, Formosa, China and some fabulous countries reported by the Asiatics at Malacca. It seemed to him that there existed a vast and legitimate field for Spanish enterprise. Its exploitation was sooner or later inevitable and he determined to be the exploiter. . . . Magellan undoubtedly betrayed his natural allegiance. . . . The world in hailing him as one of its great men, has tacitly agreed that honour was well lost.   [pp 185–6]

That is as maybe, but the King of Spain gave him authority to proceed on 22 March 1518; the expedition, however, took a long time to prepare and it was not until

67

20 September 1519 that he sailed from San Lúcar and headed for Tenerife in the Canaries. It was his declared purpose to reach the Moluccas by sailing westward and finding 'a south-west passage' into the Pacific even if to do so he had to reach down into the Antarctic circle; and if in the end there proved to be no such passage, he was to about ship and go to the Moluccas via the Cape of Good Hope; but one way or the other, he was to grab off the Moluccas for Spain.

With him went a Lombard named Antonio Pigafetta whose account of the expedition, *The First Voyage round the World*, is a classic of the period. Pigafetta was interested in everything and his book is at this point the most detailed record of such a voyage ever made while it was in progress.

Magellan had five ships. They were:

San Antonio	120 tons	*carrying about*	50 men
Trinidad	110 tons	*carrying about*	60 men
Concepción	90 tons	*carrying about*	40 men
Victoria	85 tons	*carrying about*	40 men
Santiago	75 tons	*carrying about*	30 men

Between them the ships mustered a total of 234 men and they were stored for a two-year voyage. How advanced they were in design on the caravels of da Gama or the *Santa Maria* of Columbus it is difficult to say but an illustration in De Bry's *Americae III* of 1592 shows them as round-hulled, flat-sterned, heavily armed vessels with high-piled fore and after castles. They have three masts, square-rigged on fore and main and lateen-rigged on the mizzen. There are square topsails on fore and main and the high-tilted bowsprit carries the contemporary development of the *artemon* sail first encountered in the Alexandrian grain ships of the Romans.

The little fleet took only six days to Tenerife, but by then Magellan was already at odds with some of his officers and had been tipped off that they intended to mutiny. Adopting a policy of massive inaction, he pushed on past Cape Verde and then had a row with Juan de Cartegena, master of the *San Antonio*, about his lack of proper respect for himself as commander. He had little luck with the wind and spent sixty days backing and filling in the doldrums before he got a favourable slant. There was another run-in with Cartegena during this period and this time Magellan relieved him of his command.

A landfall was eventually made near Pernambuco where they bartered with the natives for fresh provisions and thought they did well out of the deal:

For one fishhook or one knife, those people gave five or six chickens; for one comb, a brace of geese; for one mirror or one pair of scissors, as many fish as would be sufficient for ten men; for a bell or one leather lace, one basketful of potatoes. These potatoes resemble chestnuts in taste and are as long as turnips. For a king of diamonds which is a playing card, they gave me six fowls and thought that they had even cheated me. . . .

[Pigafetta, quoted by Sanderlin, pp 42–3]

Continuing to the southward Magellan came to Rio de Janeiro where he spent a couple of weeks and then in due course to the mouth of the Rio de la Plata, the great river already discovered and partly explored in 1515 by Juan Diaz de Solis. It was in Magellan's mind that this great estuary was the strait he was seeking and he sent the *Santiago* in to confirm it while the rest of the fleet groped about along the south shore. He is reported to have been 'bitterly disappointed' when the *Santiago* came back with the news that the great gulf led only into a freshwater river, and it needed all the confidence and strength of personality he could muster to persuade his crews to continue to the south.

Continue they did and on 31 March 1520 entered Port St Julian in 49½ degrees south where they stayed for five months and saw out the bleak southern winter.

For Magellan it was a desperate time. From the start the crews were for giving up the project and heading back north into the sun and they can hardly be blamed. Already they were on short rations and home-sick, and the lowering skies and freezing cold of this God-forgotten spot took out of them what heart they had left. The inevitable result was mutiny which broke out on 1 April and came within a hair's-breadth of succeeding. Three of his five ships were immediately taken over by the mutineers headed by Cartegena and another of the captains, Gaspar de Quesada, and the plan was to attack Magellan's own ship, the *Trinidad*, next day.

But the renegade Portuguese was tough and never more dangerous than when cornered. He was cornered now with a nucleus of like-minded men who remained true to him; and he stalled while he schemed and worked out an elaborate plot to regain control. His plan involved blocking the harbour mouth with one of his loyal ships and then taking the mutinous ones on singly and recapturing them by surprise. It worked like a dream and his vengeance was savage and swift. Quesada was beheaded; the body of Luis de Mendoza, killed in the fighting, was quartered and the pieces spitted on poles set up on the shore; and Cartegena, the ringleader, was marooned on a desolate stretch of coastline together with a priest who was in on the mutiny.

That appeared to sew up the troublemakers but it was by no means the end of

29 Holbein's ship (*c.* 1532) illustrating a further stage in the evolution of the three-masted, square-rigged ship. Note drummer and fife-player right aft, men hoisting mainsail, others carousing in maintop and one being sick over side

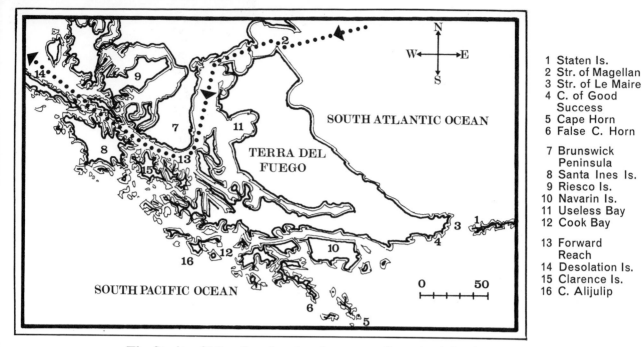

30 The Straits of Magellan showing the passage from the Atlantic
into the Pacific

Magellan's sorrows and his next set-back was the loss of the *Santiago* which tore her bottom out on a hidden shoal while reconnoitring the coast to the southward.

That was on 22 May by which time Magellan knew that he had been swindled by the ship-chandlers in Seville who, by juggling with the receipts, had supplied only half the quantity of food signed for. Instead of a whole year's supply he had less than six months' left. This startling fact he somehow kept entirely to himself and did what he could to make good the deficiency by salting down local fish and sea-fowl.

St Julian in the end became too much even for Magellan and on 24 August he shifted his ships to an anchorage in the mouth of the Santa Cruz river in 50 degrees south latitude. There he stayed for two more months spending most of the time fishing for the pot; then lured by a promise of spring in the air on 18 October the four ships pulled out and heading still to the southward immediately ran into a howling gale.

It must have seemed like an ill omen but only three days later – 21 October 1520 – they came to a headland round which lay the strait they were seeking. The day was the *Feast of the Eleven Thousand Virgins* and that was the name they gave to the cape 'because of that very great miracle. . . .'

> . . . Had it not been for the captain-general we would not have found that strait, for we all thought and said that it was closed on all sides. But the captain-general who knew where to sail to find a well-hidden strait, which he saw depicted on a map in the treasury of the king of Portugal, which was made by that excellent man, Martin Behaim, sent two ships . . . to discover what was inside the cape of the bay;
>
> [Pigafetta, quoted by Sanderlin, p 76]

which shows a touching faith in Magellan but fails to explain how Martin Behaim got to know about it.

That headland is still called Cape Virgins to this day. It lies in approximately $52\frac{1}{2}$ degrees south latitude and from it the channel runs westwards to a point known as the First Narrows where its width is down to less than a mile. The next stretch heads south-west to the Second Narrows which is about seventy miles from the entrance. From there the channel turns southward and widens out again to almost fifteen miles. Then comes Cape Froward which 'is the southernmost point of the mainland of America, almost on the 54th parallel', and the half-way mark of the passage. From there the course runs north-west by west to the Pacific end of the channel at what Magellan called Cape Deseado which is now known as Cape Pillar.

Magellan had a grim experience feeling his way through this labyrinth and it took him thirty-eight weary, heart-breaking days to do it, during which time the *San Antonio* deserted him and turning about, headed back for Spain; but he made it and on

> . . . Wednesday, November 28th, 1520, we debouched from that strait, engulfing ourselves in the Pacific Sea. . . .   [Pigafetta, quoted by Sanderlin, p 89]

And now the route west-about to Cipangu was no longer a cosmographer's dream. It lay open to the world.

There is still much to be told about Magellan but his first sight of Cape Deseado was the culmination of that period of continuously intensified voyaging which added a whole New World to the map and gave trade and commerce, ships and shipping, the biggest boost they have ever known. For in spite of treaties and bulls and all the political manipulation involved in them, these voyages were basically commercial enterprises; they were expected to show a profit and dozens of ship-masters and merchant venturers were lined up ready to sail in the wake of every one of them. Although the traders were often bloody-minded, their memory made shameful by the enslaving of simple people and their efforts concentrated on the acquisition of precious metals and stones, it was by no means a one-way business. Pohl, quoting from Herbert I. Priestley's *History of American Life*, lists what the Old World gave to the New:

> . . . wheat, barley, rye, some beans, chick-peas, lentils, almonds, mulberries, cherries, walnuts, chestnuts, medlars, tulip trees, linen, flax, indigo, alfalfa, canary seed, quinces, apples, apricots, most of the pitted fruits (not plums), oranges, limes, lemons, citron trees, cedars, pears, rosemary, willows, broom roses, lilies, old-fashioned flowers, sugar cane, bananas (some varieties), tamarinds, mangoes, grapefruit. Arabian horses from Andalusia and various kinds of seeds were sent to the northwest in 1509. The *Casa de Contratacion* successfully sent almonds, figs, cherries, pomegranates and quinces, kept on the decks in half barrels filled with earth. . . .

And in addition to the treasure and the slaves, the New World gave to Europe:

> . . . corn, chocolate, coffee, tomatoes, 'Irish' potatoes, and Lima beans; many kinds of fruit such as cassava, guava, papaya and avocado; alpaca wool, mahogany and many other valuable woods; the turkey, quinine, rubber. . . .   [Pohl, p 194]

The biggest contribution of all, however, was to the persecuted and dispossessed of the Old World. To them it gave good earth on which to build again and with it the promise of freedom.

71

The North-west Passage

1 JOHN CABOT (1450–98)

THUS, OF THE THREE ROUTES WESTWARD to the wealth of the Orient dreamed up in the 15th century by cosmographers, traders, shipless sea-captains and plain adventurers anxious to stake their worthless lives on an outside chance of fame and fortune, one had been proved and opened up by Magellan and another – the middle or tropical route – demonstrated by Balboa and the Spaniards on the Isthmus of Darien to be non-existent. That left the third proposition – a way north-about between the northernmost extremity of the American continent and the roof of the world. This became known as the *North-west Passage* and though it went on luring clear-sighted men, as well as the desperate and foolhardy, to death and disaster for 500 years; though in the end it was indeed proved to exist, it never became a viable route for ship-borne trade; moreover it never could because of the severity of the climate in the region and the permanent ice that lies across it. But the seafarer clings passionately to his dreams; to him what might be is always more attractive than what is; and in consequence the North-west Passage became the most desperately and persistently pursued illusion that ever plagued him.

The man who may be said to have started it all was a seaman adventurer named Giovanni Caboto, better known as John Cabot.

John Cabot was born at Genoa in 1450, but subsequently moved to Venice and became a naturalised subject of that city-state. He is listed in the record quite starkly and simply as the 'discoverer of North America', and is credited with being the first to attempt to reach India by the North-west Passage.

As a seaman, Cabot was involved in the spice trade and it is a fair assumption that he voyaged not only to La Tana and Alexandria but even got as far as Jiddeh in the Red Sea. There he must have met and talked with eastern merchants and ship-masters and learned from them that the spices they carried originated in islands beyond the eastern extremities of the continent of Asia; and there it must have occurred to him that these islands could be reached much more quickly and easily by sailing to them westward across the Atlantic; and that their priceless products could be brought back to Europe the same way and without paying tribute to the various middlemen and strong-armed potentates along the existing eastern route.

With this idea stewing in his mind, he started looking for patrons and backers, a search that brought him to London during the 1480s with his wife and three sons, Sebastian, Lewis and Sancio. For a while the family lived in Blackfriars but presently moved to Bristol where the merchants and people with money had the reputation of being more forward-looking and game to take a chance. He was there when the news of Christopher Columbus's first voyage broke and that seems to have sprung the balance for him. Four years later, he received letters patent from King Henry VII 'for the discoverie of new and unknowen lands'.

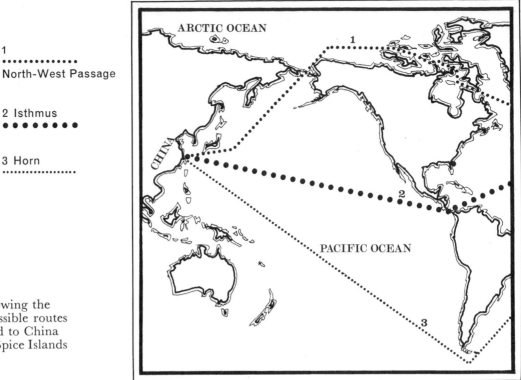

1
••••••••••••
North-West Passage

2 Isthmus
● ● ● ● ● ● ●

3 Horn
••••••••••••••••

31 Map showing the
    three possible routes
    westward to China
    and the Spice Islands

The authority, granted 'to our welbeloved John Cabot citizen of Venice, to Lewis, Sebastian, and Santius, sonnes of the sayd John' and signed by the King on 3 February in the thirteenth year of his reign, was

> . . . to take six English ships in any haven or havens of the realme of England, being of the burden of 200 tunnes, or under with all necessary furniture, and to take also into the said ships all such masters, mariners, and subjects of the king as willingly will go with him. . . .
> [Hakluyt, v. 84]

In return for the licence Cabot bound himself, his sons and their heirs to pay the King a fifth of all the profits he might make from the enterprise.

Compared with Columbus and Vespucci, John Cabot's requirements were staggeringly modest and on 2 May 1497 he left Bristol in the bark *Matthew* manned by his son Sebastian and seventeen other men mostly belonging to the port. Some of the latter were merchant venturers and Williamson reckons not more than a dozen were seamen. Of the ship herself nothing much in the way of record survives except that she first appears in the Customs Records of the port in 1503–4 when she made voyages to Ireland, to Bordeaux and finally cleared for Spain with 'William Claron as master. . . .' She was most likely a small, full-rigged ship, decked and designed for deep-water sailing.

Expressly bound by the terms of his licence not to cross the Atlantic in a southerly latitude because such a course would conceivably give offence to Spain and Portugal, Cabot, after clearing the Channel and the south coast of Ireland, 'bore towards the north' for some days then steered west. On 24 June, fifty-four days out from Bristol, he made a landfall, never conclusively identified but generally assumed to have been the westernmost point of Cape Breton Island.

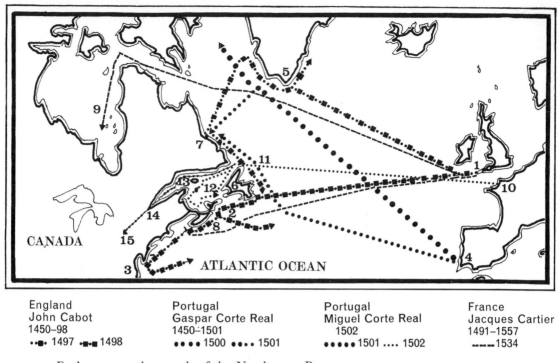

England	Portugal	Portugal	France
John Cabot	Gaspar Corte Real	Miguel Corte Real	Jacques Cartier
1450–98	1450–1501	1502	1491–1557
··■· 1497 ·■·■ 1498	●●● 1500 ●●●● 1501	●●●●● 1501 1502	----1534

32   Early voyages in search of the North-west Passage

Cabot had no doubt that the cape he had discovered was on the mainland of Asia; not the part known to Marco Polo but a wild and undeveloped region far to the north-east of the cities. He sailed along the coast far enough to confirm its south and westerly trend, then put about and headed for home. They found no gold or spices, but noted what in the end was probably more important for their fellow men. The waters through which they voyaged were alive with fish. 'Infinite quantity of fish,' records a map of the period, 'sturgeons, salmon, very large soles a yard long, and many other kinds of fish, and the greater number of them are called *baccalaos*' (i.e. cod).

They were back in Bristol on 6 August and John Cabot immediately went on to London to report to the King, who gave him £10 from the Privy Purse and promised him a life pension of £20 per annum.

Fantastic claims were made for Cabot's voyage by the newsmongers of the day. One had it that he had found the fabulous Seven Cities; another that he had discovered 'the country of the Grand Khan' and the King had 'promised him a fleet of ten ships with which to sail next spring and the services of all the convicts in the jails to perform the hard labour of the expedition' (Williamson, p 171). Meanwhile in London Cabot was the lion of the hour.

> He is called the Great Admiral, and vast honour is paid to him, and he goes dressed in silk, and these English run after him like mad, and indeed he can enlist as many of them as he pleases and a number of our rogues as well.
>
> [Pasqualigo, quoted by Williamson, p 171]

At this point John Cabot becomes the subject of much controversy and there is a great deal of confusion about him and his son Sebastian who is often credited with the second voyage made in 1498. There is confusion also about John Cabot's thinking. Believing that on his first voyage he had discovered the north-eastern extremity of Asia, there would be no point in him trying to get round it to the northward on his second. Such a course to his mind could only lead back to England. Yet when he did sail it was north-west he headed, 'not expecting to find any other land than that of Cathay and from thence to turn towards India' (Sebastian Cabot, quoted Newton, p 135).

That was in May 1498 and the expedition consisted of two ships provisioned for a year. Hakluyt says:

> And in the company of the said ship, sailed also out of Bristow three or foure small ships fraught with sleight and grosse marchandizes, as course cloth, caps, laces, points and other trifles. . . .   [v. 90–1]

They made their landfall on the coast of Greenland north of Cape Farewell and began to experience great difficulty with their compasses due to magnetic variation. There was also the cold to contend with and finally the ice in the shape of both bergs and floes. At the price of enormous effort and great suffering they reached the latitude of 67·30 degrees north in the Denmark Strait and there the crews gave up the struggle and refused to take the ships farther. This left Cabot with no option but to turn back and he headed south and west looking for the land he had sighted the previous voyage and also for Cipangu. On the second leg of the voyage, Cabot crossed the Davis Strait (between Greenland and Baffin Island) and raised the coast of Labrador in latitude 57·30 north. Turning south from there he crossed the entrance to Belle Isle Strait which he took to be a mere bay, coasted eastwards round Newfoundland then south and west along the coast of Maine to 'the latitude of Gibraltar' (i.e. 36 degrees N.). At this point, Cipangu continuing to elude them and with their stores running dangerously low, they had to call it a day and head for home.

Commercially the voyage was an abysmal failure. The ships arrived in Bristol empty of spices, jewels, gold, even slaves, and those who had backed the voyage lost everything they had staked.

2 THE CORTE REALS

It was to be several years after that before any more English money could be raised for such risky ventures. Spain and Portugal, however, were doing very well out of their seafaring. By this time – AD 1500 – the fact that the lands discovered in the course of the search for a western route to Cathay and Cipangu formed a whole new continent must have been recognised, and the search for the North-west Passage had become a definite objective. From now on men sailing out of Europe to the westward, headed north, not vaguely because of political pressures, but purposefully and knowing precisely what they sought.

The next one up into the ice was a Portuguese from Terceira in the Azores, João Fernandez by name. Nothing much is known of his achievements but he was followed quickly by another Azorean, a nobleman called Gaspar Corte Real. Corte Real sailed from Lisbon with two ships in the early summer of 1500 and, heading north, made a landfall on the east coast of Greenland. He kept on up the Denmark Strait until he ran into impassable ice, then turned back and doubling Cape Farewell groped some distance up the west coast. There is no record of the latitude he reached and it is only known that he got back to Lisbon safely before the end of the year.

On this voyage Williamson says:

> The Greenland shores were sufficiently forbidding to discourage any plans for their exploitation, and the fact that Corte Real returned to them is a sign that they possessed another attraction. This can only have been that there was hope of a passage past them to Asia. [p 202]

Corte Real appears to have been so seized up with the idea that he could hardly wait and the spring of 1501 saw him pushing north and west again. It was a bad year for ice and he failed to touch the coast of Greenland because of it; but he drove on westward to Labrador, then followed the land southwards, crossed the Straits of Belle Isle and arrived on the coast of Newfoundland. There he grabbed off sixty Indians as slaves, sending them home in two of his ships. With the third ship, he headed south and was never heard of again. So the North-west Passage as such claimed its first victim and there were many more to follow.

When Gaspar Corte Real failed to return, his brother Miguel took out 'a patent to continue the discovery'. That was in January 1502 and on 10 May that year he left Lisbon with three ships. Miguel kept well to the south of Cape Farewell and made his landfall on Newfoundland towards the end of June. Here his ships split up after arranging to get together again on 20 August. Two of them made the rendezvous on time but the third with Miguel Corte Real himself aboard failed to show up and was never seen or heard of again.

Thus the Portuguese bid for the North-west Passage failed; but it was far from being a dead loss.

> If there was no Asiatic passage established there was at least something valuable in Newfoundland – the fishery, the long timber suitable for spars, and the natives who, it was thought, would make good slaves. Portugal had hitherto obtained her spars in Europe, and the largest were brought by the Hanse traders from the Baltic, a voyage quite as costly as that across the Atlantic. With the new Indian Ocean traffic demanding big ships, a Newfoundland producing-area was worth consideration.
>
> [Williamson, p 203]

3   SEBASTIAN CABOT (c. 1474-1557)

The next big name to crop up in connection with 'that murderous quest, the North-west Passage to the Indies' (Rose, p 97) is Sebastian, son of the Genoa-born, Venetian-naturalised, Bristolian John Cabot who had died in the meantime. No seafarer of the period has created so much confusion and controversy about his achievement as Sebastian. He finished up Pilot-major of Spain and made a notable voyage to South America, but all the accounts of his early days are bedevilled with *ifs* and *buts*. Some commentators have even called him 'a vainglorious liar'; and 'It has been said that he suppressed his father's fame and appropriated his achievements' (Williamson, p 230).

His voyage to the North and West is generally dated 1508 and he is reputed to have had two ships and a company of 300 men; and Williamson suggests that if he had anything like this number the majority of them were colonists and '... that he proposed to plant a settlement somewhere on the route to Cathay' (p 240). He considers the figure an exaggeration and thinks it extremely unlikely that 'Sebastian ... would have launched into the unknown with a crowd that he could not feed for more than a few weeks' (p 240).

All that, however, is by the way. He sailed and made a landfall in the vicinity of Cape Farewell, then headed up the Davis Strait where it is claimed for him he reached $67\frac{1}{2}$ degrees north latitude. This must have taken him through Hudson Strait into Hudson Bay and at that point he believed he was actually in the Pacific, and the sea ahead of him was open all the way to Cathay. But he could go no farther; his crews were too badly worn with hardship and exposure to go on and he was compelled to turn south again, '... discovering every bay, river and creek to see if it passed to the other side'. It was his hope to find a more temperate passage and when this failed to show up, he returned to England to find Henry VII dead and his patronage gone. Three years later he went to Spain and though he was reduced to drawing maps for two marks a time, in the end he won the interest of the Queen and entered her service.

4 JACQUES CARTIER (1491–1557)

After Sebastian Cabot's failure there was some talk of sending him out again to Cathay by the north-west in 1521. It came to nothing and the next known attempt at the passage was made in 1527 by an English captain named John Rut. He too failed and seven years later the French took up the search. Their dreamer was a Breton, Jacques Cartier, born in St Malo in 1491.

33 Sebastian Cabot. By S. Rawle

34 Jacques Cartier. By Dan Lailler

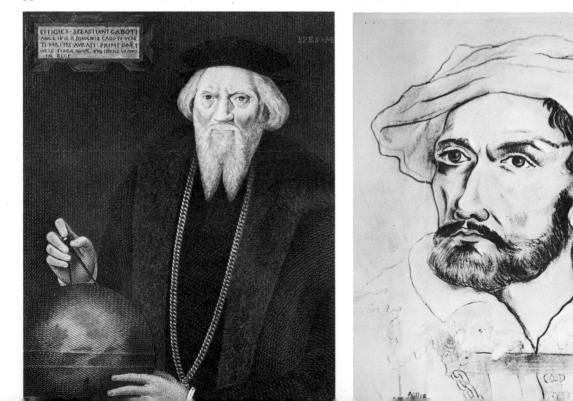

In 1534 he sailed from his birthplace with two ships 'with intent to find the North-west Passage to Japan' (*Everyman's Encyclopedia*, iii. 132) and arrived at Cape Bonavista early in May. He found the coast of Labrador so bleak and forbidding that he characterised it as 'the land God gave to Cain'; and turning southward, he felt his way down the west coast of Newfoundland into the Gulf of St Lawrence. Still groping, he entered Chaleur Bay (between Quebec and New Brunswick) and for a little while thought he had found the way only to be disappointed again. Coming back into the Gulf he pushed northward to Anticosti Island but though the passage on the far side of it looked full of promise, the current flowing seaward through it was so strong his ships could make no headway against it and eventually he had to give up and head for home, arriving at St Malo on 5 September.

Nothing daunted, Cartier set out again the following year and this time got as far up the St Lawrence as Quebec. From there he went on in longboats reaching the site of the modern city of Montreal on 3 October. The rapids of Lachine then barred his way and while held up there he apparently heard something that put the North-west Passage out of his mind. Newton says:

> His object, however, like that of Cortes and Pizarro, seems to have been to find gold and he received at Hochelaga the impression that up the river Ottawa there existed a mysterious kingdom of Saguenay, rich in jewels and precious stones. . . .   [p 144]

He was safely back in France by the summer of 1536 and made a third voyage five years later, this time in search of the fabulous Saguenay. It was a disaster and many of his people were killed by the Indians. Nevertheless France owes him a great debt for he gave her Canada,

> . . . a bequest comparable with that of Columbus; for while the Genoese bequeathed to Spaniards mainly treasure, the Breton handed on to his countrymen a homeland.

[Rose, p 99]

5 SIR MARTIN FROBISHER (*c*. 1535–94)

In spite of the toll it had already taken in ships lost without a trace, seamen drowned, frozen to death or miserably wiped out with scurvy, the North-west Passage to China continued to haunt the minds of men and the next big name on the roll is an Englishman, Sir Martin Frobisher, born in Yorkshire about 1535.

Frobisher was no courtier, no noble sprig dicing with death on the high seas for the excitement and the odd chance of fame and fortune. He was an honest-to-God seaman and had made his first voyage in the Guinea Trade before his twentieth birthday. Then throughout the next ten years he sailed annually on voyages along the North African coast into the Levant.

He was forty-one when he sailed from the Thames on his first voyage in search of the North-west Passage. His fleet consisted of two *barks* (presumably similar to Cabot's *Matthew*) – the *Gabriel* and the *Michael* – and a pinnace. The master of the *Gabriel* was Christopher Hall and Hakluyt's account of the voyage is built up out of extracts from this seaman's log. It is the flat-footed, undramatic record typical of the seafarer, completely unemotional and entirely factual. He notes down their departure from

35   Martin Frobisher.
By C. de Passe

Gravesend on 12 June 1576, observing that the latitude was 51 degrees 33 minutes and the compass variation $11\frac{1}{2}$ degrees. Twelve days later the entry reads:

> The 24. day at 2. of the clocke after noone, I had sight of Faire yle, being from us 6. leagues North and by East, and when I brought it northwest and by North, it did rise at the Southernmost ende with a little hommocke, and swampe in the middes.   [v. 132]

Any detail that might be of use on subsequent voyages or to other voyagers is noted down meticulously – soundings, the nature of the bottom, the run of the tides, the weather, courses sailed, compass variation and so on. Thus running into Fowlay (Foula) between Orkney and Shetland he writes:

> I found my elevation to be 37. degr. and my declination 22. degr. 46. min. So that my latitude was 59. degr. 46. min . . . and there did ancre in seven fathoms water, and faire sand. You have comming in the sounds mouth in the entring 17. 15. 12. 10. 9. 8. and 7. fathoms and the sound lyeth in North-north-west. . . .   [v. 132]

Further on he records a sounding of fifty fathoms 'and streamic ground, like broken otmell, and one shell being redde and white like mackerell'.

From Foula Frobisher made a course a little to the north of west. It was a wild, stormy passage with the wind mainly south to south-west and the ships running before it. On one day the master records 'we had so much winde that we spooned afore the sea. . . .' But it was a quick passage for those times and on 11 July they made a landfall, since identified as being in the vicinity of Cape Farewell.

Immediately they encountered ice which along with persistent fog and very strong shifting tides plagued them mightily while they were in the region.

79

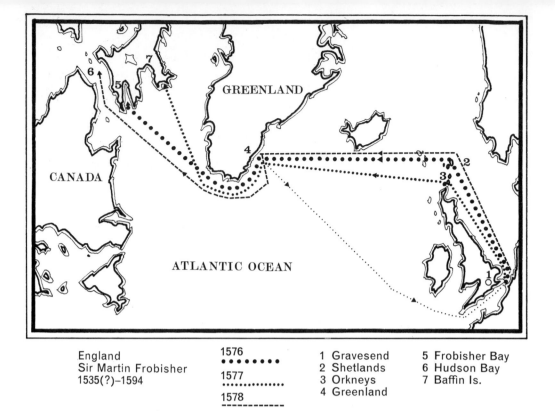

England
Sir Martin Frobisher
1535(?)–1594

1576 • • • • • • •
1577 • • • • • • • • • • •
1578 - - - - - - - - - -

1 Gravesend
2 Shetlands
3 Orkneys
4 Greenland

5 Frobisher Bay
6 Hudson Bay
7 Baffin Is.

36 Sir Martin Frobisher's three voyages in search of the North-west Passage

Pushing on regardless, Frobisher came to a grim ice-bound coast which he assumed to be Labrador and groped northward along it. Then on 11 August he entered what he took to be the desired strait leading to the Pacific. The strait, however, was really a bay running into Baffin Land and since labelled with Frobisher's name. Probing on, they made contact with the Eskimo, described by Hall as '. . . like to Tartars, with long blacke haire, broad faces, and flatte noses, and tawnie in colour. . . .' (v. 136); but in the end the ice defeated them and they were forced to turn back without discovering the head of the bay.

The passage home began on 26 August and it was as wet as and much more weary than the outward run. They encountered heavy pack ice off the Greenland coast and on 7 September

> . . . we had a very terrible storme, by force whereof one of our men was blowen into the sea out of our waste, but he caught hold of the foresaile sheate, and there held till the Captaine pluckt him againe into the ship. [v. 137]

They raised Orkney on 25 September and reached Harwich safe and sound on 2 October.

The Queen herself, says Heawood, named the new land *Meta Incognita*, or the *Unknown Bourne*, in the highly romantic spirit of the age.

With high hopes Frobisher made a second voyage the following year and Hakluyt has his record of this one from 'Master Dionise Settle.' This time he had three ships – the *Aide*, of 180 tons or thereabouts, and the same two *barks* as on the previous voyage, i.e. the *Gabriel* and the *Michael*. He was

. . . accompanied with seven score Gentlemen, souldiers, and sailers, well furnished with victuals, and other provision necessarie for one halfe yeere, on this his second voyage, for the further discovering of the passage to Cathay and other Countreys, thereunto adjacent, by West and Northwest navigations; which passage or way, is supposed to bee on the North and Northwest part of America: and the said America to be an island invironed with the sea, where through our Merchants may have course and recourse with their merchandize, from these our Northernmost parts of Europe, to those Orientall coasts of Asia, in much shorter time, and with greater benefite than any others, to their no little commoditie and profite that do or shall frequent the same.   [v. 138]

which puts the whole theory of the North-west Passage and the economic reasons for seeking it into a single sentence, even if it is a long one!

He made it back to Frobisher Strait and again the ice was bad, and of all the company only Frobisher seems to have been undaunted by it. When the ships could proceed no farther he went on in small boats. Four days later a shift of wind dispersed the heaviest of the ice and the way into the bay was open to the ships. Further discoveries were then made, and one inlet was named Jackman's Sound after his Master's Mate. It was in this vicinity that he saw an outcrop of black rock which '. . . sparkled and glister(ed) in the Sunne like gold. . . .' Thinking it was indeed gold, he loaded both his ship and the *barks* with the mineral, counting on it to cover the expenses of both his voyages and yield a handsome profit besides.

Turning homeward on 24 August, the little fleet was dispersed by '. . . occasion of great tempest and fogge'; but Frobisher raised Land's End on 17 September and went on to Milford Haven. One of the *barks* arrived at Bristol on 29 August and the other, after running round the north of Scotland, made Yarmouth safely on the 31st. They lost all told only two men – 'one in the way by Gods visitation' (most likely exposure when they were in the ice) and the other washed overboard on the way home.

The black stones were reported to contain gold and a company was promptly formed to exploit the discovery. In 1578 Frobisher sailed again to the North-west but no longer seeking the passage to Cathay. This time he had miners and soldiers with him

37   Cod fishing in Newfoundland.
Detail from a map of 1698
printed in *Histoire de la
Découverte de la Terre*
by Larousse

and his intention was to establish a settlement on the shores of Frobisher Bay. There were fifteen ships in the expedition and in heavy weather one was lost and the others badly damaged. The project was abandoned but not before the ships had been loaded up with the black stones. On 31 August they started homeward and arrived in the Thames around the end of September.

There it was learned that the black stones were worthless, the glittering particles being mere iron or copper pyrites, and the bubble burst. The shareholders lost every penny they had put up and Frobisher himself was reduced to poverty.

From this point it could be argued that although the underlying motive remained purely commercial and therefore closely linked with ships and shipping, the search for the North-west Passage moved out of the sphere of seafaring as such. True the expeditions were backed and often promoted by groups of *Merchant Venturers*, one of which ultimately became *The Company of Adventurers of England trading into Hudson's Bay* and as such exists most powerfully today; but the men who commanded the expeditions were becoming more and more *explorers* and less and less simple seamen. The work demanded other qualities and different skills, and the need threw up generation after generation of dauntless, dedicated men whose names are household words – John Davis, Henry Hudson, William Baffin and later Alexander Mackenzie, John Franklin, Captain F. W. Beechey, with, later still, Ross and Parry, McClintock and McClure and Greely; and in modern times, Nansen and Amundsen, the Scandinavians.

It seems a long time for men to chase a dream, but though the direct results proved in the end to be almost purely negative there were positive benefits for mankind on the side.

> These voyages were of great value to commerce, for both Hudson and Barents reported such quantities of whales and walruses that the waters were soon thronged with whalers from every maritime nation.   [Croft, p 3]

And the Grand Banks fisheries, the timber of Newfoundland, the wheat and beef of the Canadian prairie states are really by-products of the killing search for the North-west Passage.

The Circumnavigators

THERE IS SOMETHING about the very idea of circumnavigating the globe that still stirs the heart and fires the imagination of the least web-footed and the most irrevocably chair-bound mortals. To have done so is today the common experience of thousands – tourists, civilian aircraft pilots, merchant-navy crews and defence personnel – and gimmickry has been introduced to make the feat more sensational or hazardous. One man tries it land-hopping in a jeep or on a bicycle; another goes in a catamaran and a third challenges empty sea and sky single-handed; so it seems only a matter of time now before somebody does it in a row-boat or on a raft. Way back, however, using all the resources available and making it as simple, as easy as men knew how, it was the biggest gamble ever undertaken; and it came off only at the cost of unimaginable suffering and hardship.

Magellan was the first and he it was who proved it possible. Then came Drake and after him a handful more. None of them was concerned with records or out to create a sensation. They were after a quick profit with no scruples about how they made it; and any fame that subsequently accrued to them was incidental. Nevertheless, they added immensely to man's knowledge, enhanced enormously his potential wealth, improved incalculably his ultimate condition, and the part they played in the history of seafaring was crucial.

1 MAGELLAN

As noted above, on 28 November 1520 Magellan made history by entering the unknown and hitherto only vaguely anticipated ocean by the Straits that now bear his name; and even if he guessed the Moluccas were still half the world away the fact cannot have mattered much to him then. He called on the priest to bless the ships and led the crews in chanting a *Te Deum*, then fired off his guns for the sheer joy of it. There were many in his company ready to call it a day, among them notably the astronomer, Andrés de San Martin, who suffered bitterly from the cold and was dead against the exhausting business of sailing at night, but the captain-general was going on and nobody could stop him. Addressing his officers he is reputed to have said:

> . . . we now are steering into waters where no ship has sailed before. May we always find them as peaceful as they are this morning. In this hope I shall name this sea the *Mar Pacifico*.
> [quoted Sanderlin, p 89]

His hopes about the weather were by and large fulfilled, and that was just as well because he had little good fortune otherwise. Pigafetta says:

> . . . We were three months and twenty days without getting any kind of fresh food. We ate biscuit which was biscuit no longer but a powder full of worms. . . . We were forced

to eat the hides with which the main yard was covered to prevent chafing against the rigging. . . . We had also to use sawdust for food and for rats we paid half a ducat apiece. . . .
[quoted Newton, p 192]

Practically everybody, except surprisingly Pigafetta, became ill in some degree with scurvy and nineteen died on the passage from the disease. They made daily runs of fifty, sixty, or even seventy, leagues but sighted no land except two desert islands that afforded no anchorage, let alone relief; and the Lombard wrote:

When we left that strait, if we had sailed continuously westward we would have circumnavigated the world without finding other land than the Cape of the Eleven Thousand Virgins.
[quoted Sanderlin, p 91]

which gives some idea of how amazed he was by the vastness of the Pacific Ocean.

The fact of the matter is that their ships were unsuitable for such prolonged passages. They carried insufficient quantities of the basic necessities in food and fresh water. The living quarters they provided were tolerable for short voyages but totally inadequate for long ones, being cramped, dark and damp – circumstances which bore heavily on the spirit after a time, and with the effects of the vitamin deficiency in the diet and the uncertainty not only about the outcome of the passage but even about what the next day or the very next hour might bring, combined to create psychological tensions leading to the deep depression so symptomatic of scurvy. Then there was the clumsiness of the gear and the great weight of the sails which because of the still quite primitive design of the hull needed constant trimming to maintain headway. This made the labour of the seamen not only arduous but incessant and a weary body had little resistance to the dreaded disease. In the end only a truly tough character, inured to suffering and steadfast in purpose, could survive. For the others apart from the physical symptoms such as progressive weakness, loosened teeth and falling hair, depression led to apathy, apathy to despair, despair to surrender and surrender to death. Newton sums it up:

The shipping of the 16th century had barely reached the stage of development when with infinite suffering and heroism the Pacific could just be crossed. . . . The hardihood displayed by the pioneers of the early period has never been surpassed, but they paid dearly for immortality.
[p 192]

From Cape Deseado (Cape Pillar) Magellan headed north, most likely looking for the sun to dry out his ships and drive the cold out of the bones of his crews. He appears to have hugged the coast for something like 1,500 miles which brought him into the latitude of Valparaiso on 16 December 1520; then he altered course to west-north-west and drove on into the blue. According to one account, he crossed the Line in 165 degrees west longitude and Pigafetta notes that on the way they had considerable trouble with magnetic variation. He would know little or nothing about easting and westing, the usual practice at this time being to navigate '*by altura*' which was a process of determining latitude by Pole Star or sun and running along it.

On the assumption that this was Magellan's method, he could not have been heading for Ptolemy's Cape Catigara which was reputed to be in $8\frac{1}{2}$ degrees south latitude nor for the Moluccas which are on the Equator because he stood on until he was about 900 miles north of the Line, then headed west along the 13th parallel. It is suggested he was going for what are now called the Philippines, the latitude of which he must have learned along with tales of their incredible richness in gold during a voyage east from Malacca.

The first landfall (apart from the two rocks noted above) came on 6 March 1521. It was in the group now known as the Mariana Islands. He, however, named them *Islas de los Ladrones* (Islands of Thieves) because the natives of them, swarming round his ships in outrigger canoes, stole everything that was not nailed down, including a small boat off the poop of the flagship.

Weak as his men were, Magellan would not let this pass. He took forty heavily armed men ashore, burnt forty or fifty houses and many boats, and killed seven men. He also got his boat back and pushed on.

Then at daybreak on Saturday, 16 March, they sighted the island of Samar in the Philippines and

> The following day, the captain-general desired to land on another island which was uninhabited and lay to the right of the above mentioned island, in order to be more secure, and to get water and have some rest. He had two tents set up on the shore for the sick and had a sow killed for them. [Pigafetta, quoted by Sanderlin, p 102]

Contact with the natives' rulers quickly followed and Magellan would seem to have been most anxious to impress them with his power. It is estimated he had only about 150 men left of his company and many of them were sick. To prove their superiority, perhaps even to create a legend that they were invulnerable, he had one dressed in full armour attacked by three others with sword and dagger. He was struck on all parts of the body but remained unhurt and 'thereby was the king rendered almost speechless'. Then, according to Pigafetta, the captain-general boasted that one of his armed men was worth a hundred of the natives, and that he had 200 of them in each ship.

That was in the island of Limasaua from where Magellan went on past Leyte, Bohol, Canigao and Gatighan to Cebu, which he had heard was the wealthiest and most densely populated island in the group. He arrived there on 7 April and sailed in with banners flying and all his guns firing to make sure he created the right impression.

The King had it in his mind to demand tribute from the ships but a Moorish merchant there told him what the Portuguese had done to Calicut and Malacca, and the guns helped him to think better of it. He even embraced Christianity, accepted baptism for himself, his queen and 800 of his people, and changed his name to Charles, prefixing it with Rajah to mark his rank. But when he began burning the idols of his people, some of them revolted against him.

Magellan's response to this was more burning and killing. The trouble-makers were concentrated on the neighbouring island of Mactan and the captain-general determined to bring them to heel. There is some evidence that he saw the conflict as an opportunity for demonstrating in actual battle the immeasurable superiority of the Spaniards and the invincibility of Christian weapons. He went in with forty-eight men, few of whom were really fit. Against them, Pigafetta, who was one of the forty-eight, reckons they had at least 1,500.

The battle was joined and though the Christians burned and slew with the utmost zeal, they were slowly driven back into the water. There Magellan was wounded in the arm and being unable to draw his sword to defend himself was slashed across the left leg with a scimitar.

85

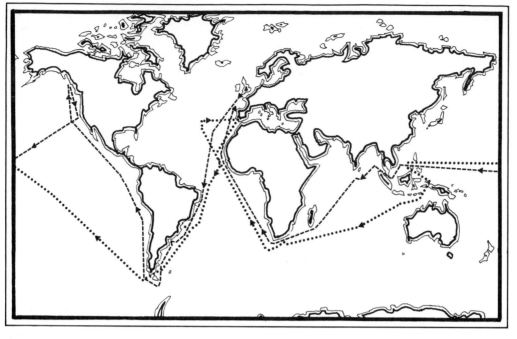

Portugal 1519
Ferdinand Magellan
1480–1521
Lisbon, Canary Is., Cape Verde Is.
C. St Augustine, Rio de Janeiro,
St Cruz River
Tierra del Fuego, Philippines, Mactan

England ------------------ 1577–80
Sir Francis Drake
1540–96
Brazil, Rio de la Plata, Cape Horn
Vancouver Is., Philippines, Spice Is.
Indian Ocean, Cape of Good Hope

38   The routes followed by the circumnavigators, Magellan
     and Drake

> That caused the captain to fall face downward, when immediately they rushed upon
> him with iron and bamboo spears and with their cutlasses, until they killed our mirror,
> our light, our comfort, and our true guide.   [Pigafetta, quoted by Sanderlin, p 133]

That was the end of the affray sometimes dignified with the name of the *Battle of Mactan*.
The Spaniards had lost eight killed beside their captain and only the boat-guard among
the rest were not wounded in some other way than merely in their pride. The most
serious casualty, however, not even excepting the commander, was the reputation of the
voyagers. Gods they might be but it was known now beyond a doubt that they had feet
of clay.

The Rajah Charles reverted, enticed a party of twenty-four men ashore from the
ships then turned on them. Only two escaped and under the command of one Carvalho
the ships slipped their moorings and sailed away, leaving the others to suffer whatever
fate 'the Christian King' had in store for them.

At this point the survivors of the expedition numbered 115, which means that
slightly more than half of those who had sailed from Seville had been left dead, dying
or deserted on the way. The *Concepción* was stripped and burnt and in the *Trinidad* and
Victoria 'We stowed the best of its contents . . . then laid our course toward the south-
south-west. . . .'

86

The basic aim of the voyage – to find the Moluccas and annex them for Spain – had still to be achieved; and trapped as they were in the maze of the eastern archipelago, it was months before they sighted their ultimate goal. First they went to Borneo and looked in at Brunei where Pigafetta was much impressed by the elephants and the crowded shipping – mostly junks.

> That city is entirely built (over) salt water, except the houses of the king and certain chiefs. It contains twenty-five thousand fires. The houses are all constructed of wood and built up from the ground on tall pillars. When the tide is high the women go in boats through the settlement selling the articles necessary to maintain life.
>
> [quoted Sanderlin, p 146]

A town on stilts and so is much of it today.

Somewhere along the north coast of Borneo the ships were careened, caulked and generally overhauled. Here also Carvalho was relieved of his command and replaced by Espinosa with Sebastián del Cano, who had been involved in the mutiny at Port St Julian, as captain of the *Victoria*.

Still the Moluccas proved hard to find and it was not until 8 November 1521 that they finally dropped anchor in the harbour at Tidore. They were then only forty-eight hours short of twenty-seven months out from Spain.

The voyagers were well received at Tidore and also at Ternate, the other famous port in the Moluccas, and after a long round of ceremonial and festivities, they got down to the task of finding a cargo. It was cloves they were after and Sanderlin reckons the standard measure – a *bahar* – weighed 406 pounds. According to Pigafetta their trade goods brought into the ships cloves at the following rate:

> Red Cloth, 18 yards for one bahar; Hatchets, 15 for one bahar; Glass drinking cups, 35 for one bahar; Cinnabar, 23 pounds for one bahar; Quicksilver, 23 pounds for one bahar; Linen, 48 yards for one bahar; Knives, 150 for one bahar; Scissors, 50 pairs for one bahar; Caps, 40 for one bahar;

39 Ferdinand Magellan. A painting in the National Library, Madrid

and so on. He adds: 'Our haste to return to Spain made us dispose of our merchandise at better bargains to the natives than we should have done' (quoted Sanderlin, p 161).

When at last the time came for sailing, it was decided to divide forces, the *Trinidad* to recross the Pacific north of the Line to Darien and the *Victoria* going on south and west to double the Cape of Good Hope and complete the circumnavigation. Pigafetta fails to make the purpose of this manœuvre clear but the hostility of the Portuguese may have had something to do with it. In effect the expedition challenged their supremacy in the area and threatened their monopoly of the spice trade; and the voyagers had learned in Ternate that the King of Portugal had already sent one fleet to the River de la Plata and another to the Cape of Good Hope with orders to intercept and destroy the Spanish ships and their renegade Portuguese commander. Perhaps it was thought that by splitting up they would stand a better chance of evading their enemies.

In the event the *Trinidad* made a very poor showing, springing a leak and almost drowning all hands before she could get her anchor off the bottom. It was obviously going to be a big job to make her seaworthy and the *Victoria* could not hang about waiting for her if she was to take advantage of the Monsoon, so at noon on 21 December 1521 the *Victoria* finally left Tidore with sixty hands aboard all told including '13 Indians'. The rest of the surviving personnel – fifty-four including Juan Carvalho – elected to stay on to attempt the Pacific crossing when the ship was ready. The *Trinidad* did in fact sail in April 1522, heading east; but bad weather, hunger and scurvy drove her back to the Moluccas where the Portuguese caught up with the remnant and threw them into prison. Newton records that two-thirds of their number had already perished and 'of the rest only four survived captivity and returned to their native land' (p 196). He continues:

> Not until 1565 did Andres de Urdaneta discover the correct course and season for sailing and by so doing establish the Spanish trade route from Asia by way of Central America to Europe. Prior to that date a number of Spanish captains crossed the Pacific to the Asiatic islands but not one of them retraced his course. [p 196]

Meanwhile the *Victoria* took all of fifty days to thread her way through the islands and it was not until 11 February 1522 that she came clear and headed west-south-west from the coast of Timor, leaving Sumatra to the north 'for fear of the King of Portugal'. To double the Cape of Good Hope she reached down to 42 degrees south latitude and was held up there for nine weeks by contrary winds and storms. She got round it at last on 6 May, then ran north and west for two months during which time twenty-one of her people died.

Driven by the stark necessity to survive, they put in at the Cape Verde Islands, out of food, short of water, the hull worm-eaten and leaking like a basket, the foremast gone and rigging and gear alike rotten to the edge of uselessness. They learnt here that they had also lost a whole day on the way which puzzled them more than somewhat, Pigafetta declaring: 'I had set down every day without any interruption.' The disturbing thing about this was that for half the voyage they had been observing the holy days quite wrongly and also eating meat on Fridays.

The Portuguese were friendly at first and gave them succour, even helping them to step a new foremast, but when they learnt where the *Victoria* had come from they turned nasty and grabbed a boat with thirteen men aboard. At this the commander slipped his anchor and got out before worse befell them. Nevertheless the stop at the Cape Verdes was their salvation and on Saturday, 6 September 1522, the ship with only 18 left of the 234 who had sailed with the expedition entered the Bay of San Lucar. Thus was the first circumnavigation of the world in a single ship finally accomplished. Three years it had taken and only one of the five ships in the expedition had made it; but her cargo of cloves is estimated by Sanderlin to have been worth 675,000 dollars and the venture showed a very handsome profit for its backers.

Summing up the results of Magellan's voyage, Newton says:

> First it revealed the Pacific Ocean in its true magnitude, as may be seen from the official Spanish map drawn by Diego de Ribero in 1529 and embodying mainly the knowledge gained by Magellan. . . . Secondly it gave to Spain a footing in the Far East (the Philippines). By means of it the Spaniards exploited a share in the trade of Asia, operated a regular trade route across the Pacific and played a worthy part in the earlier stages of the exploration of that ocean. [p 197]

2 SIR FRANCIS DRAKE (c. 1540–96)

Any appraisal of Sir Francis Drake is likely to be more subjective than reliable. Even in his lifetime opinions about him differed. Simple people who feared God and tried to keep his commandments looked on him as a bloody-minded pirate; others distrusted rather than condemned what he did because it could lead to war with Spain; and some, more closely involved maybe, deplored and resented the disastrous effect of his actions on sea-borne trade. Now he is seen either as a national hero, part of the English folklore, a symbol, a legend or a cold-hearted, murdering, rapacious and calculating thief, depending on the viewpoint and basic values of the observer. Stow, a contemporary, declared in his *Annales* that Drake was 'ambitious for honour' and 'greatly affected to popularity . . . as famous in Europe and America as Tamburlaine in Asia and Africa' (quoted Gibbs, p 10). Drake himself, however, had no difficulty in squaring off what he did with his conscience. With his mouth at least he was pious, embracing the Protestant creed and detesting the Pope and all things Papist. This hatred, focusing itself on the Spaniards, was his justification for all his actions.

He was half a century after Magellan and in the interval Spain had got the exploitation of the wealth of Central and South America extremely well organised. She had established ports in Chile, Peru and on the Pacific side of the Isthmus; places like Valparaiso, Coquimbo, Arica, Callao and Panama. There she was building ships in which to sail the treasure of gold and silver up to the strip of land joining the two sub-continents, whence it was carted by mule train across the narrows to Nombre de Dios, then loaded into other bottoms to cross the Atlantic to Spain. So too with the equally valuable products of the Spice Islands. In 1529 her conflict with Portugal for the control of this trade had been partly resolved by the Treaty of Saragossa which fixed the dividing line between the two countries at $297\frac{1}{2}$ leagues east of the Moluccas; then in 1543 she proved strong enough to disregard the agreement and annexed the Philippines. By 1565 she was seriously colonising these islands and her ships were regularly crossing the Pacific on the Trade winds.

Nombre de Dios proved to be an irresistible lure to Sir Francis Drake. It was there in 1572–3 with only two small ships and seventy-three men, that he ambushed and looted a treasure train heading into the town from Panama; it was off the port in 1596 that he died, not of Spanish steel in his vitals nor of a Spanish bullet in his brain, but of unheroic dysentery, stinking and robbed of human dignity, while he was still too young to go; and it is there, if the poet is to be believed, that he still lies:

> . . . in his hammock and a thousand miles way,
> Slung atween the round shot in Nombre de Dios Bay
> And dreaming all the while of Plymouth Hoe.

It was on this earlier raid that he saw the Pacific and worked out the plan for the subsequent voyage. He argued that because the coast had been so long an exclusive Spanish preserve the shipping along it was unarmed and the ports they used unfortified. Once he got into the Pacific the treasure of all Chile, Peru and Mexico would be his for the taking, to say nothing of the spices.

He apparently had little trouble in getting backing for his project though at the time England was at peace with Spain. Queen Elizabeth herself is reputed to have put in a stake and there were a number of other big names in the subscription list. Gibbs suggests it is extremely unlikely that the Queen gave Drake any formal commission. All of them knew whose corns they were proposing to tread on and significantly Hakluyt begins his account of the voyage as follows:

The 15 day of November, in the yeere of our Lord 1577. M. Francis Drake, with a fleete of five ships and barkes, and to the number of 164. men, gentlemen and sailers, departed from Plimmouth, *giving out his pretended voyage for Alexandria.* . . .   [viii. 48]

Such a pretence could only have been made (*a*) to establish an alibi for the Queen and the other high rankers in the plot and (*b*) to fool the Spaniards and prevent them mounting a pre-emptive strike against the expedition.

The ships were:

Pelican, 100 tons (afterwards renamed *Golden Hind*); *Marigold*, 30 tons; *Swan*, 50 tons; *Elizabeth*, 80 tons; *Benedict*, 15 tons (this is described as a pinnace).

All were heavily armed with sixteen to eighteen guns in each of the bigger ships besides smaller calibre firearms and hand weapons. There were fourteen boys in the company which included about a dozen gentlemen adventurers. The mariners, according to Gibbs, were on wages and the gentlemen on shares. From the beginning the position of the gentlemen appears more than a little ambiguous. As Gibbs puts it:

They were not exactly officers serving under a superior officer and by birth and education most of them had the advantage of Drake, the nature and extent of whose own authority were open to question. These were matters which would have to be settled in practice – and not inconceivably by violence.   [p 26]

Among the gentlemen was one Thomas Doughty who had met and become a close friend of the seaman while he was lying low in Ireland after the Nombre de Dios affair.

The start of the expedition was not too happy, for the ships immediately ran into heavy weather and sought shelter in Falmouth.

41   Queen Elizabeth I. By Marc Geerarts. This is the painting known as the Armada Portrait with scenes of that great battle in the background. Original at Woburn Abbey

... where such and so terrible a tempest tooke us, as few men have seene the like, and was in deed so vehement, that all our ships were like to have gone to wracke: but it pleased God to preserve us from that extremitie, and to afflict us onely for that present with these two particulars: The mast of our Admirall which was the *Pellican*, was cut over boord for the safegard of the ship, and the *Marigold* was driven ashore and somewhat bruised. ...
[Hakluyt, viii. 48]

Putting back to Plymouth to refit, they finally left the Sound on 13 December and made their first landfall on the coast of Morocco twelve days later, which was Christmas Day. Pushing on they reached Mayo in the Cape Verde Islands on 28 January 1578, wreaking considerable havoc on such fishing vessels and Portuguese caravels as they met with on the way.

In the Cape Verdes the islanders took to the hills at the very sight of the English and let them get on with it, which they did, laying in all the fresh food and water they could stow. From Mayo they moved on to St Thiago and there Drake took the Portuguese ship *Maria* bound for Brazil with a cargo of wine, linen and woollen cloth and other commodities. She was found to be a good prize and 'she yeelded unto us good store of wine'. Drake decided to keep the ship and put Thomas Doughty in command of her with a sailing-master under him. He also kept the pilot, a man named Nuno da Silva, of whom more will be heard later.

The voyagers obviously found the Cape Verdes a pleasant place to linger in and before they took their departure they had a look at Fogo and also the Ilha Brava; but the business of the expedition came before any other consideration and on 2 February the ships stood out to sea and headed for the Rio de la Plata.

It was fifty-four days later on 5 April that they made their next landfall, which was on the coast of Brazil in latitude 33 degrees south. It was a testing passage for everyone,

42 Drake's fleet at Santo Domingo, 1585. England was at war with
Spain. Drake sailed to the West Indies and took the cities of
Santiago (Cape Verde Islands), Santo Domingo, Cartagena
and St Augustine

including as it did three weeks becalmed, 'great stormes, terrible lightnings and much thunder'.

Another 400 miles brought them into the mouth of the River Plate where they stocked up with seal-meat and water then pushed on after stripping and abandoning the *Swan* and the prize taken in the Cape Verdes. On 20 June, just over six months out from Plymouth, the four remaining ships arrived at Port St Julian where the most prominent feature was apparently Magellan's gibbet, still standing against the sky.

Perhaps it was an omen; maybe it created an atmosphere of distrust and betrayal; or it could be that a show-down between Drake and Doughty just had to come. Come it did; Doughty was accused and subjected to a form of trial in which Drake seems to have been judge, jury and chief witness for the prosecution; then condemned; and beheaded after receiving communion. Hakluyt records that 'our Generall himselfe accompanied him in that holy action', which might be considered as a wholly unnecessary piece of hypocrisy on Drake's part.

This execution of Doughty has never been satisfactorily explained and it remains probably the darkest blot on the Admiral's much bespattered memory. He was the most distinguished and influential of the gentlemen adventurers and Drake owed him for favours he could never return in kind. It is even suggested that their relationship was one of client and patron rather than of simple friendship and Drake just had to be supreme. Gibbs sums it up as follows:

> On the whole therefore it is a fair conclusion that Doughty came to appear to Drake in the light of a rival, all the more dangerous because in many respects (not necessarily germane to the enterprise) he had the advantage of him. In the second place there is reason to believe that Doughty shared the view . . . that the expedition had no business with the Straits and the Pacific but should have sailed for the West Indies. . . . [p 39]

It was not until 17 August that Drake took his departure from grim Port St Julian and before he did so another ship was abandoned, reducing the fleet to three, namely the *Pelican*, the *Elizabeth* and the *Marigold*. Three days later on the 20th (though the kidnapped pilot, Nuno da Silva, reckoned it was the 24th) they were into the Straits of Magellan. It was here for some reason that Drake changed the name of his flagship to *Golden Hind*.

The three ships made an easy and uneventful passage of the Straits. It turned out to be the fastest one in the 16th century and took only sixteen days; but they got all that was coming to them at the other end. Entering the Pacific at Cape Pillar on 6 September and heading north-west, they met with extremely heavy weather that continued almost without a break for two whole months. During that time both the *Marigold*, carrying a crew of twenty-eight, which foundered with all hands on 30 September, and the *Elizabeth*, which parted company and headed back through the Straits for home on 21 November, were lost to Drake. He also lost a pinnace with seven men aboard, one of whom incredibly survived and got back to England via Brazil, taking eight long years to do so.

Meanwhile the *Pelican* under her new and more elegant name of *Golden Hind* had been driven so far to the southward that her people saw the turbulent conjunction of Atlantic and Pacific oceans south of Cape Horn. One way and another it was not till the end of October that they were able to head northward again, and get down to business.

Their first call was at Valparaiso where they looted the church and seized the only ship in the harbour. Gibbs reckons the plunder here was more than enough to cover the cost of the expedition and Hakluyt records that they rifled the ship at sea.

> . . . and found in her good store of the wine of Chili, and 25,000 pezos of very pure and fine gold of Baldivia, amounting in value to 37,000 ducats of Spanish money and above. . . . [viii. 59]

But this was nothing to what was still to come.

At Coquimbo they lost a man in a skirmish with 500 Spaniards (if Hakluyt is to be believed) and then, landing at Tarapaza, found a man asleep with thirteen bars of silver by his side. '. . . we tooke the silver, and left the man'.

Pushing on, picking up bars of silver and bags of it wherever they touched, they came via Arica to Lima where there were twelve defenceless ships in the unfortified harbour. These were rifled and yielded much of value, but the biggest thing Drake got in Lima was the news that a treasure ship called the *Cacafuego* was just ahead of him up the coast making for Panama.

He set off in pursuit and a fortnight later came up with her. She too was unarmed and could make no resistance. He took her after bringing down her mizzen mast with his third and last shot; and

> . . . we found in her great riches, as jewels and precious stones, thirteene chests full of royals of plate, foure score pound weight of golde, and sixe and twentie tunne of silver. . . .
> [Hakluyt, viii. 60]

It took six days to transfer the *Cacafuego*'s treasure to the *Golden Hind*, after which she was turned loose to make the best of her way to Panama.

By this time the whole Pacific coast was alerted to Drake's presence, frantically arming itself and devising methods of countering his ruthless raiding. The looting of the *Cacafuego* was the last straw and word went forth that at all costs he must be prevented from leaving the South Sea with his plunder. The Straits of Magellan were blockaded and strong forces deployed along the Isthmus of Darien in case he tried to take a chance overland.

Drake was much too shrewd a character not to anticipate these moves. He reached the port of Guatulco at the beginning of April, plundered it, then headed seaward leaving behind him Nuno da Silva, the Portuguese pilot, to take his chance with the Spaniards. This, like the execution of Doughty, seems to have been an act of gratuitous cruelty, and is another dark place in his memory.

By this time his ship was foul in the bottom and leaking badly, so he found a deserted island where he could lay her aground for the necessary overhaul; and it was here, as likely as not, that he made up his mind about his course home. As Hakluyt puts it:

> Our Generall at this place and time, thinking himselfe both in respect of his private injuries received from the Spaniards, as also of their contempts and indignities offered to our countrey and Prince in generall, sufficiently satisfied, and revenged: and supposing that her Majestie at his returne would rest contented with this service, purposed to continue no longer upon the Spanish coasts, but began to consider and to consult of the best way for his Countrey. [viii. 62]

There were three ways open to him; he could run the Spanish blockade and go back through the Straits of Magellan; he could strike northward and achieve undying fame by finding the fabulous North-west Passage back into the Atlantic; or he could run on to the westward via the Moluccas and the Cape of Good Hope. He chose the last of these alternatives which makes his ultimate circumnavigation a matter of expediency, the desperate resort of a much-hunted man.

Gibbs has it that after leaving Guatulco he disappeared entirely from the view of both his own countrymen and the Spaniards until he reached home waters eighteen months later; but from Hakluyt it is possible to trace his course.

From 16 April till 5 June he ran to the northward, which was the recognised custom of the Spanish ships bound for the Philippines, the object being to get into the region of the north-east Trade winds. At the end of that spell he had sailed 600 leagues and was in latitude 43 degrees north, the hands suffering grievously of the cold. It could be argued that up to this point he was aiming for the North-west Passage and, realising if he continued the cold would become increasingly severe, only then opted for the longer but easier west-about course via the Moluccas and the Cape of Good Hope. Turning back, however, he made a landfall in 38 degrees north on what is now the coast of California; and, after indulging a little more his fancy for fire and sword and terrifying the inhabitants, he named the land New Albion and annexed it for England.

Leaving this place on an unspecified date, he headed west and, after encountering several groups of islands on the way, finally reached the Moluccas on 14 November. Here Drake kept his guns silent and appears to have been welcomed kindly; here too he picked up a cargo of cloves – the only commercial transaction the whole voyage could boast.

Pushing on, the *Golden Hind*, which incidentally was sheathed against the teredo worm, was careened in the Celebes and then on 9 January 1579 ran aground on a hidden reef.

Her plight seemed desperate but Drake rose to the occasion and – probably more to the point – his incredible luck held. He lightened the ship by unloading on to the rocks three tons of cloves, eight big guns and a few other items, and then 'the winde (as it were in a moment by the speciall grace of God)' shifted and drove her clear.

A little time was now spent in Java; but being warned that other ships were in the vicinity and presumably not wanting to have to answer too many questions about the treasure below his hatches, 'our Captaine would stay no longer. . . '. They sailed, making a course south and west and their next landfall was the Cape of Good Hope. Like the Straits of Magellan, the stormy Cape of old Bartolomeo Dias was kind to them and Hakluyt describes it as

> . . . a most stately thing, and the fairest Cape we saw in the whole circumference of the earth, and we passed by it the 18. of June.   [viii. 74]

The next stop was at Sierra Leone on 22 July. There they took aboard fresh water and provisions and, sailing on the 24th, made an incredibly long passage to arrive back in England on 3 November 1580, almost three years after leaving.

Given the last word on the voyage, Lewis Gibbs says:

> Considered purely as a feat of navigation Drake's voyage round the world was notable without being spectacular . . . (it) was not made for the sake of the exploit . . . it was made because he had the wit to see that it was the best way home and the resolution and resource to act on that conclusion.   [p 6]

And whatever one may think of Drake as a man, that seems a fair enough comment on his achievement as a seafarer.

95

Terra Incognita Australis

1 THE LURE OF THE GREAT SOUTH LAND

AS NOTED IN AN EARLIER CHAPTER the idea of a great land-mass south and east of Africa had been in men's minds since before the time of Christ and a number of legends like that of the lost continent of Atlantis sprang from it. The urge to go looking for this South Land seems to have developed out of the travels of Marco Polo for he initiated the quest not only for Java and the Spice Islands but also for 'a great continent beyond . . .' (Rose, p 124). His story was that about 500 miles south-west of Java was a great country which he called Locach or Beach.

> . . . It was on the mainland and around it was land abounding in gold; while at the same distance beyond was an island named Pentam; and then 100 miles farther still, a very rich island called Java the Less. [Rose, p 126]

The work of seafaring peoples of all nations during the 16th century had increased enormously the positive knowledge of the globe and a number of ancient false premises and misconceptions had been corrected or abandoned. America for instance was now known to be neither small in area nor to stretch across the North Pacific in a low latitude to join on to eastern Asia. It was recognised as a separate continent, a whole New World. But along with that other mad dream of a commercially usable channel round the top of America, men continued to cling to the belief in a Great South Land.

The voyage of Magellan, far from disproving the concept, had even strengthened it in some minds for it was easy to believe that the land to the south of his Strait, i.e. Tierra del Fuego, was part of a huge continental mass. The belief was further strengthened in 1563 by a Spanish pilot running between Chile and Peru. He was Juan Fernandez, after whom the beautiful island off the South American coast is named. Fernandez claimed he had been set to the westward in about latitude 40 degrees south and there had found a great land

> . . . very fertile and agreeable, inhabited by white people, mighty well disposed, of our stature, well clothed, peaceable and civil. . . . [Rose, p 127]

On his return to Chile, he kept the whereabouts of his great discovery a secret, hoping to return in due course and claim it. He died, however, before he could do so and his secret was buried with him. Nevertheless this story was taken for gospel truth by the believers in the Great South Land right down to the end of the 18th century.

> It seems incredible apart from the supposition that this land formed part of a continent to the west of Juan Fernandez which has been submerged. This theory has found supporters, the chief being the late Dr. Macmillan Brown in his *Riddle of the Pacific* (Easter Island). . . . [Rose, p 127]

The Spaniards were still seeking this fabled continent at the beginning of the 17th century. Then the Dutch had a go and after them the French, who tried very hard and

96

got little to show for their pains. In 1739 one of their seamen, Pierre Bouvet, on a voyage dedicated to the search, driving south-south-west from the Cape of Good Hope, sighted a towering headland in latitude 55 degrees south and assumed it was the northern tip of the Great South Land. It proved to be no more than a barren rocky island since named after him. Thirty-odd years later another Frenchman, Yves Joseph de Kerguélen-Trémarée, usually known as Kerguélen for short, made a search in the southern Indian Ocean. He was looking for 'a fertile southern land' reported by de Gonneville of Honfleur over 150 years before. He too sighted land which he claimed was part of the lost continent and reckoned would give France control of the sea-route to the East Indies and allow her to dominate the spice trade. But this was also a dream and his discovery is now known as Kerguélen, a group of islands scattered over the area between 38 and 50 degrees south and 70 to 80 degrees east longitude. They are so inhospitable as to be barely habitable and virtually their only useful product is the *Kerguélen Cabbage* which whalers on long passages used to call there for as a preventative of scurvy.

This dream of *Terra Incognita Australis* was so vivid and persistent in the minds of men that demands were constantly being made for new efforts to find it. In 1756, for example, de Brosses, a Frenchman, basing himself on ancient Ptolemy, pointed out that nothing at all was known of the South Pacific and demanded that France should acquire the unknown lands there. Doing so would give her world supremacy for 'he who is master of the sea is master of the land' (quoted Rose, p 185). Then in 1766 a Britisher named John Callender called on his country's seafarers to make these vast potential resources their own; and Alexander Dalrymple, a Scottish seafaring merchant familiar with the East Indian trade, went to the trouble of compiling a survey of all the discoveries made in the Pacific Ocean up to 1764. One of his rather wild assertions was that the Great South Land had already been discovered on its east side by Juan Fernandez and on its west by the Dutch under Tasman. All that remained was to find the bits in between and he promised that the whole would comprise '. . . a greater extent than the whole civilised part of Asia, from Turkey eastward to the extremity of China' (Rose, p 186).

Then in 1772–4 James Cook spent three whole years seeking this dream of Ptolemy. Navigating with consummate skill and daring, he reached as far south as 70 degrees 10 minutes, and circumnavigating in these high latitudes, exploded the myth once and for all, as shall be seen.

It might be thought strange that with so much discovery going on throughout the 15th and 16th centuries the South Pacific should remain virtually unknown until the 18th; but there were objective reasons for this, facts of life pulling against the visions of the dreamers. In the first place it must be remembered that discovery for discovery's sake came in at a very late date. Indeed even today's exploration of outer space, although presented as being in the interests of science, has economic and political implications which make it impossible for the great nations to pool their resources and ideas; and it is doubtful if there has ever been such a thing as absolutely uncommercial and disinterested exploration. The motive was much more openly commercial in the early days, however, and the number one priority for men like Columbus, Cabot, Vespucci and Magellan, to say nothing of old Bartolomeo Dias and Vasco da Gama, was to show a profit on their voyages. Moreover the bigger the profit, the greater the honour accruing to them and the easier it became to get the backing for another trip.

These men were not explorers except incidentally; they were seafarers and merchant venturers pushing their luck. They looked for new lands, new ports, new markets and new sources of raw materials because it was in these that the cream lay thickest; and scores of unsung heroes sailed quickly in the wake of every one of them, eager to skim off what was left. So the Great South Land had to wait while there was a softer option with a quicker and surer profit elsewhere.

Out of this general basic idea, J. Holland Rose adduces three clear reasons for the long delay in opening up the South Pacific. First there was the extremely difficult passage through the Straits of Magellan or round the Horn. The prevalent westerly winds made a ship battle desperately for every mile of westing she gained and by the time she was into the Pacific she was

> . . . generally so battered . . . and crews were so weary and scorbutic that further struggles westward were unthinkable and sails were gladly set for a run northwards towards more genial climes. [p 186]

Like Magellan's men all they wanted was to feel the sun on their backs again. Thus it was that the voyagers all stood away to the northward from the Straits instead of heading west. Secondly there were the currents, notably the northerly drift named after Humboldt. Feeling that sweeping him along after all the weary weeks of backing and filling the ship-master wanted nothing more than to sit back and let it, even though it was taking him to the north. Besides, he knew that the quicker he got north of the Line the quicker he would pick up the north-east Trade winds and the faster time he would make to the Spice Islands. Finally

> . . . The precious metals of Peru and Mexico also tempted seamen northwards either to work them or to plunder the vessels that bore the bullion from Acapulco to the Philippines and on to Spain. Thus Nature and man's greed limited him, during some 150 years, to certain well-marked Pacific routes and relegated the south of that vast expanse to the domain of vain conjecture or political jealousy. [Rose, pp 186–7]

As shall be seen, political manipulation, aggressive nationalism, oppression, commercial expediency and plain greed are all elements in the story, but first a look at the ships and the art of running them in that period.

2 DEVELOPMENTS IN SHIP DESIGN, NAVIGATION AND INSTRUMENTS IN THE 17TH AND 18TH CENTURIES

After the rapid advances in design initiated by Henry the Navigator and stimulated by the requirements of the search for a way to the Indies in the 15th and early 16th centuries, there was a period during which new ideas were tried out in practice and modified until true seaworthiness was achieved. That this level had been reached was demonstrated in Drake's circumnavigation of 1577–80 when, as the Andersons point out, '. . . he went from Java to Sierra Leone, at least 8,500 miles, without touching at any port on the way' (p 135).

In detail the changes that can be noted by the end of the 16th century were the introduction of stern and quarter galleries, a longer hull, higher ends and gun-ports.

43   Developments in ship design in
17th and 18th centuries.
1 Bobstay; 2 Dolphin striker or
Martingale boom; 3 Whipstaff;
4 Elaborate decoration of stern and
Quarter galleries; 5 Gunports;
6 17th-century sail pattern;
7 18th-century sail pattern

The rig remained practically unchanged in so much that though a fourth mast was sometimes added and experiments were made with extra topsails, ships were, broadly speaking, three-masted, square-rigged on fore and main and lateen-rigged on the mizzen. The great eye-catching change had nothing to do with seaworthiness or sailing qualities. It was the increase in the amount of decoration. On this the Andersons say:

Decorations had perhaps increased, for ships of Elizabeth's reign had all their upper works painted in bright colours and striking patterns; but it had by no means reached its height. That came in the next century when the art of the woodcarver was employed to such an extent that ships became more beautiful than at any time before or since.
[pp 138–9]

There was little basic change during the 17th century and the designers appear to have concentrated on the perfection of existing ideas. Merchant ships remained small and resisted such changes in rig as the mizzen topsail and staysails. The reasons for this must have been economic. Smaller ships required smaller crews and showed bigger profits; also they could nose into shallower ports and even lie closer inshore to load cargoes where there was no port at all. But small crews needed the simplest rig to handle and were opposed to more topsails and staysails. So the average merchant-man of the period would spread a pattern of canvas consisting of only six sails – sprit-sail, foresail, fore-topsail, mainsail, main topsail and lateen mizzen. The *Mayflower* of the Pilgrim Fathers was such a ship.

In warship design there were no such inhibiting factors. This was the period of Samuel Pepys and Phineas Pett, and when it came to ships these two never thought small. In 1637 Pett built the *Sovereign of the Seas* with a high, *round-tuck* (as distinct from square) stern and beak bow. She was a three-master with royals on fore and main and a topgallant sail on the mizzen which would make her a bit of a moon-raker for her time.

From this time on, i.e. *c.* 1650, there is more certainty and much less speculative thinking about our knowledge of ship design. Wooden scale models were now being made and of these, one of the *Prince*, built in 1670, survives in South Kensington with an earlier one still in Stockholm. Artists too were finding a lucrative field for their talents in drawings of ships and those of the Van de Veldes, father and son, are particularly interesting (*vide*, Andersons, pp 148–9).

Such changes as did take place during the 17th century were evolutionary rather than revolutionary and are summed up by the Andersons as follows:

Compared with the ship of 1594 that of a hundred years later had a markedly straighter hull. In rig the obvious changes are at either end of the ship, the fixed spritsail and the spritsail topsail on the bowsprit and the single mizzen with a square topsail in place of the two mizzens with a lateen topsail to one of them. . . .   [p 159]

44   Detail from a contemporary paint-ing by Abraham Storck depicting incidents from the naval action between Dutch and English, 1 to 4 June 1666. This shows very clearly the lavish decoration and moon-raking masts common to warships of that time

Another development, first noted in a model dated 1701 and mentioned by the Andersons, is the *bobstay*, the line that leads from the bowsprit to a point on the stem-post below the figure-head. This must have brought about an enormous strengthening of the whole system of masts and spars and it is suggested the improvement might have come in very much earlier but for the inhibiting effect of the beak-head on the thinking of designers.

Parallel with these changes there were very big and important developments in accommodation and living conditions for the crews. According to the Andersons:

> The Captain and officers were accommodated in the after part of the ship under the poop, quarterdeck and half-deck. The gunner and his mates lived in the gunroom, right in the stern below the officers' quarters. Some of the inferior officers, such as the boatswain and carpenter, had cabins against the bulkheads which shut off the forecastle and the half-deck or quarterdeck from the open upper deck. The crew lived along the covered decks between the guns and slept there in hammocks. The cook-room was at first placed in the hold amidships but was afterwards shifted to the forecastle. Ammunition and stores of various kinds had their places in the hold beneath the lower deck. . . . [pp 161–2]

With the piled-up stern burying the tiller under two or three decks, steering presented the designers with a tricky problem. It was solved at first by a device called the *whipstaff*. This consisted of a long thin pole connected to the end of the tiller by a ring and a pin. The pole passed through the deck in a pivot which allowed it to move in all directions including up and down. By pushing or pulling the end of the pole, the helmsman was able to move the tiller to port or starboard as desired. It was never a very satisfactory arrangement and utterly hopeless in a seaway, and the introduction of the steering wheel in the early 18th century must have eased considerably the physical burden on the helmsman and the strain on the nerves of the navigating officer charged with the responsibility for steering a straight course.

Other refinements in rig introduced in the 18th century and noted by the Andersons were the boom to the foot of the mizzen and the *dolphin-striker* forward. This last was a small spar jutting downwards from the end of the bowsprit. It was more properly referred to as the *martingale boom* and

> . . . its purpose was to act as a lead for a rope which held down the jib-boom in the same way as the bobstay held down the bowsprit. The reason for this was that another sail, the *flying jib*, had been introduced outside the jib, set either on a longer jib-boom or on a new spar, the *flying jib-boom*, which prolonged the jib-boom in the same way as that spar prolonged the bowsprit . . . the first evidence for a dolphin-striker belongs to 1794. . . . [p 179]

So, slowly throughout this dull century ships continued to increase in size and seaworthiness. They increased in number too to meet the demands of swiftly expanding world trade and the problems that still bedevilled the seafarer were gradually sorted out and positive steps taken to solve them. The biggest was still the accurate determination of longitude at sea and in 1714 the British Government offered a series of rewards ranging from £10,000 to £20,000 for any generally practical and useful method of finding it. They demanded that the method should be accurate to within half a degree, i.e. 30 miles, which casts some light on the chanciness of the dead-reckoning of the day.

Meanwhile Napier's invention of *logarithms* and the publication of his table of

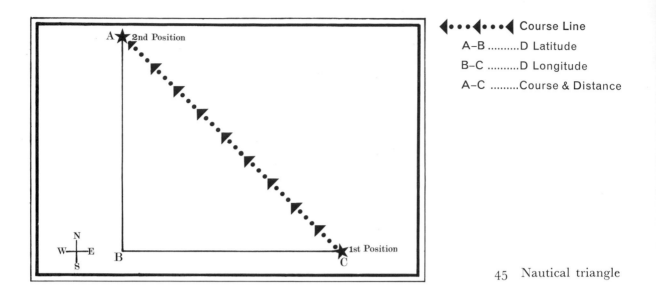

Course Line
A–B ....D Latitude
B–C ....D Longitude
A–C ....Course & Distance

log sines for every minute of the quadrant, in 1614, had enormously simplified the task of preparing accurate astronomical tables for the navigator, while the work of Gerardus Mercator had done the same for the chart-makers. The 17th-century mathematicians appear to have found navigation a fascinating and fruitful field and laboured mightily to devise new methods of using the observations of celestial bodies. There were teachers of navigation now and one of them, John Tapp, going into business as a bookseller and stationer, issued in 1601 a *Seaman's Kalendar, or an Ephemerides of the Sun, Moon and most notable fixed Stars*, which Professor Taylor says 'may be considered the prototype of the *Nautical Almanac*'. She adds:

> . . . It was written in homely style suited to poorly educated readers and contained instructions on how to use the various tables as well as rules for working out the course made good from the plain chart. [p 226]

This was done by drawing a *nautical triangle*, one side being the latitude, another the longitude and the third the course. It was a right-angled triangle and 'if two sides were known, or one side and another angle the whole triangle could be solved by trigonometry'. In 1614 John Tapp produced a table of sines, tangents and secants

> . . . and posed the six questions on the nautical triangle in what had by now become the standard way:
>
> 1. Given Difference of latitude (D. lat.) and course, what is the distance?
> 2. Given D. lat. and course, what is the departure from the Meridian? (i.e. D. long.)
> 3. Given D. lat. and distance what is the course?
> 4. Given D. lat. and distance what is the departure?
> 5. Given D. lat. and departure what is the course?
> 6. Given D. lat. and departure what is the distance? [p 227]

Using this method and these tables must have seemed sheer sorcery to the old tarpaulins and much more was still to come for them from the astronomers and mathematicians.
    Instruments were also being improved and refined. Edmund Gunter, for example,

third professor of astronomy at Gresham College who died in 1626, inscribed the logarithmic scale on the rod of the cross-staff and taught navigators how to use it with a pair of compasses to cut out tedious arithmetic. This became known as *Gunter's Line* and was so much valued by sailors that they were reluctant to 'give it up when the more convenient slide-rule was introduced in 1654'. Even the simple log-line was re-knotted in this period to make the calculating of speed easier and quicker, and by the end of the 17th century *Journals* or log-books had been formalised and tabulated so that ships in general recorded the same information in the same order. Professor Taylor quotes one set out by Abbé Fournier which had eleven columns, viz.:

1. Day and month
2. Rhumb of course
3. Wind
4. Quality of wind
5. Glasses (i.e. hours measured by hour-glass)

6. Distance
7. Estimated latitude
8. Difference longitude
9. Observed latitude
10. Compass variation
11. Accidents   [p 234]

and another dated 1696 with eight:

1. Day and month
2. Wind
3. Course
4. Distance in miles

5. Latitude corrected
6. Longitude corrected
7. Bearing of headland last seen
8. Remarkable observations and accidents. [p 235]

To this time also belong the *vernier* and the *micrometer*, both devices for further subdividing the smallest divisions of a scale, both ultimately adapted to give greater accuracy in the observation of celestial bodies.

Another tremendous boon for ship-masters was Halley's chart of the world showing lines of equal magnetic variation. This, produced in 1701, was the first isometric map 'to come into general use and its appearance was therefore a signal cartographic event, quite apart from its intrinsic value to sailors' (p 240).

So then as the years rolled by the seafarer discovered, charted and began the commercial exploitation of more and more of the habitable globe. The key to the

46   Lines of magnetic variation

N. North
magnetic pole
S. South
magnetic pole

East of True
North

West of True
North

determination of longitude at sea still eluded the egg-heads but the seaman's task was made progressively easier, his passages quicker and his landfalls surer by the work of the astronomers, the maths men and the naval architects. It was a complex reciprocating process in which necessity was the dynamic and if the story of *Terra Incognita Australis* does nothing else, it shows man, by this mustering of his resources in depth, steadily increasing his mastery over his environment.

3 THE SPANIARDS

The Spaniards were first to see the Pacific Ocean (though it was through the eyes of a Portuguese) and the first to wet their feet in it on the western shores of the Isthmus of Darien. They promptly annexed it and when the Portuguese began pushing eastwards from Java, they started feeling south and west from Panama and Peru, hoping to beat them to the Great South Land.

Their first visionary to set out in pursuit of the dream was Alvaro de Mendana, a nephew of the Governor of Peru who sailed from Callao with two ships in November 1567. According to Rose his ships were the *Capitana* of 150 tons and the *Almirante* of 107 tons, and between them they carried 150 men. He headed west-south-west and it was his firm belief, based on tales current among the Incas, that he had only 600 leagues to go before he raised the lost continent. When they had sailed this distance and nothing showed up, they altered course a little to the northward and driving on just under the Equator covered 120 degrees of longitude – practically a third of the earth's circumference – before making a landfall. Then they discovered a group of large islands lying between latitude 5 degrees and 10 degrees south. These were the Solomon Islands, but though Mendana spent six months exploring them, he found no gold and with his ships badly worm-eaten and leaking like baskets, he was compelled to head for home. He went north-about and the passage took all of eleven months to make and cost the lives of fifty of his company.

He had the bright idea of colonising the Solomons but owing partly to political jealousy and partly to the piratical activities of Drake and other Englishmen, it was not until thirty years after that he was able to make his second voyage. This time – in 1595 – he left Callao with four ships and a company that included 368 emigrants, among which number there were both women and children. His primary purpose was still to discover new sources of gold and his secondary one to find the Great South Land. In the event and largely because of the lack of a proper means of determining longitude, he failed even to find the Solomons again. He did, however, discover the Marquesas and after another long weary passage came on an island which he thought was one of the Solomons but turned out to be the island of Santa Cruz. It was here that he tried to establish his colony; it was here that greed and immorality led to violence and murder; and it was here that he died most likely of a broken heart – if such be possible.

The command of the expedition passed into the hands of Pedro Fernandez de Quiros who, strange as it may seem, was another Portuguese in the service of Spain. Quiros re-established some degree of law and order and then reluctantly abandoned the island, leading the survivors north-westwards to the Philippines whence they eventually got their ship back to the Isthmus.

Ten years later, towards the end of 1605, Quiros led another expedition out of

Peru in search of the lost continent. In the interval the mysticism that was part of his nature had developed and he had become a religious zealot. Gold was no longer the lure for him; it was souls, the souls of the myriads of people in the Great South Land that he was going to win for Christianity.

He was down to two ships again, the *Capitana* and the *San Pedrico* of 80 tons which was under the command of Luis Vaez de Torres, still another Portuguese in the service of Spain.

Steering west-south-west from Callao, Quiros sailed 800 leagues without sighting land. By this time, with supplies running low, the crews were becoming mutinous and to pacify them the course was altered to west-north-west, which was a great pity for Rose reckons if he had stood on he might well have discovered New Zealand. Instead, he reached up into better weather and running down latitude 11 degrees south, discovered Taumaco, one of the Duff or Wilson Islands lying to the north-east of Santa Cruz. There he heard of fertile and populous lands to the south and he pushed on in that direction, seeking for the 'mother of so many islands'. And sure enough, on 1 May 1606 he sighted what he believed to be the lost continent and landing there he named it *Australia del Espiritu Santo*. Then, says Williamson:

> there followed a profusion of religious ceremonies, pageants, the creation of an Order of Knights of the Holy Ghost of which every ruffian in the crew became a member, the choice of the site for a City of New Jerusalem, and then a sudden decision to call everything off and sail elsewhere. All hands embarked and the ships put to sea. . . .   [p 25]

What had happened? Had Quiros realised he was wrong about the nature of his discovery? (It turned out to be one of the larger islands in the New Hebrides.) Nobody knows; but that was finish for him. The crew got out of hand and the *Capitana* lost touch with the *San Pedrico* in a gale. Quiros was forced to sail northwards for the Philippines. In a very bad way he reached Peru and died in dire poverty at Panama in 1615. 'With him,' writes R. H. Major in *Early Voyages to Australia*, 'died the naval heroism of Spain.'

That left Torres out on his own, except for Diego de Prado, a Spanish officer, who, it might be assumed, was his second in command. Still seeking the *Terra Incognita Australis*, he pulled out from the New Hebrides and steering south-west sailed about 400 miles. Another 400 would have taken him on to the coast of Australia but once more he was turned back by the limited capacity of his ship, and with stores running short he headed for Manila. It was on this leg that he struck the south side of New Guinea and coasting eastwards passed through the strait that now bears his name, proving that New Guinea was indeed an island. Whether he also sighted Cape York remains a matter of conjecture; so far as Torres and Prado were concerned the problem was no longer to push out the frontier but simply to find a way through the maze of islands in which they had become involved and get back to the safety of Manila. They made it and that was the end of the Spanish thrust.

4 THE DUTCH

Nothing in the history of seafaring is more exciting and stimulating than the spectacular rise of the Dutch Republic. Prior to 1580 the Netherlands was a small country under the heel of, and very much oppressed by, Spain. Long before this the Portuguese had made Lisbon the centre of the eastern trade and Antwerp and Amsterdam had achieved a considerable degree of importance as distribution centres for Oriental cargoes in northern Europe. Then in that crucial year, the Dutch made a declaration of independence and decisively rejected the Spanish yoke. In response Philip II, who was ruler of both Spain and Portugal, banned the Dutch merchants from Lisbon. Faced with economic extinction, the new republic made desperate efforts to find both a north-west and a north-east passage to India. Of course they failed but the defeat of the Spanish Armada by the English in 1588 and the consequent breaking of the stranglehold which the Iberian nations between them had so long exercised on sea-borne trade, so encouraged the Dutch that in 1595 they sent a fleet to India round the Cape of Good Hope in open competition with the Portuguese.

It was a bold step and it was richly rewarded. On their second voyage in 1598, they seized the island of Mauritius and fortified it as an advance post, and a year later they were in a position to force up the price of pepper on the London market from three shillings to six and eight shillings a pound. In 1601 they formed the Dutch East India Company and by 1607 they were in full possession of the Spice Islands with factories established all the way from Persia to Japan; in 1611 they set up a post at Djakarta in Java and calling it Batavia made this the centre of their operations.

Commenting on this extraordinary development in the pattern of trade and power, Rose in an appendix says:

> The immense gains there secured encouraged them to form their well-organised Dutch East India Company (1601). Concentrating on Java and the Moluccas, it soon drove the Portuguese and English from all those islands – a proof of what could be achieved by good trade organisation, skilled seamanship and bold strokes dealt from an advanced

47 The Spanish Armada off Calais, 28 July 1588. This battle was
a decisive factor in the breaking of Spain's monopoly of
seaborne trade and the subsequent rise of the Dutch

base, Mauritius. So successful were some of the Dutch ventures that their company paid dividends of 75, 50 and 62½ per cent in the years 1607, 1610 and 1616 – gains far exceeding those of the English Company or of the Spanish treasure fleets. [p 268]

So in the end it was the Dutch who pushed south and westward from the Moluccas. The Portuguese were no longer there to do so. The Dutch also produced an early circumnavigator in van der Noort. He sailed in 1598 via the Straits of Magellan, the Ladrones and Philippines to Java and Sumatra, then on to the Cape of Good Hope and back to Holland where he arrived on 26 August 1601 with one ship left out of the four he had started with. He had little to show for it all except the ride.

The next big Dutch names are Willem Corneliszoon Schouten and Jacob Le Maire. Their voyage, far from being made under the auspices of the Dutch East India Company, was financed by a group who were trying to break that great organisation's monopoly of the eastern trade. Schouten's brief was primarily to find the Great South Land and secondly to get the richest cargo he could pick up on the way. The two ships of the expedition sailed from the Texel on 14 June 1615, making for the Pacific via the Straits of Magellan as van der Noort had done before them. In the event they passed south of Tierra del Fuego, between it and what is now known as Staten Island. This lofty coast glimpsed through the driving rain and spindrift was assumed by the navigators to be a promontory of the Great South Land. Pushing on they rounded the southernmost tip of the archipelago and named it Cape Horn after the town of Hoorn, birthplace of Schouten.

Having gained the Pacific, Schouten headed northward for Juan Fernandez to rest his crews and refit, then, striking north-west in the track of Magellan, crossed the tropic of Capricorn on 11 March. Like all the rest he was looking for the Trade winds and after a month of sailing found them in about 15 degrees south, in which latitude he continued for several weeks, discovering a few small islands but no Great South Land. The expedition finished up at Batavia where the Governor seized the surviving ship and her cargo under the terms of the East India Company's monopoly. Le Maire was shipped home and died on the way, choked with resentment it is said.

Ten years before all this, the Dutch, sailing out of the Indies, had made the first ever sighting of Australia, although at the time it was not recognised as part of a new continent but taken to be an extension of the coast of New Guinea. The ship concerned was the *Duifken* whose master was a Willem Janszoon of Amsterdam. The *Duifken* sailed from Bantam in Java on 28 November 1605. She was bound for the eastern parts of the archipelago on a trading voyage, be it noted, not a voyage of discovery. Heawood traces her course as follows:

> . . . After touching at the Ke and Aru groups the *Duifken* appears to have reached the coast of New Guinea in Latitude 5 degrees S. and to have followed the shores round Prince Frederick Henry Island as far as the beginning of the Torres Strait. Then steering south the Dutch vessel traced the eastern shores of the Gulf of Carpentaria as far as 13.45. S. having thus – for the first time so far as record exists – sighted the coasts of Australia. [p 70]

Janszoon however, as noted above, misinterpreted what he had found. He saw nine of his crew murdered by the natives while attempting to open up trade and then called it a day.

And in the end it was by pure chance that the Dutch found Australia. By 1616 their East India Company was so firmly established and so powerful, its ships sailing round the Cape of Good Hope to Java could pick their route according to the season and the prevailing winds, sure of being unmolested wherever they went; and one of them, the *Eendracht*, Captain Dirk Hartogszoon of Amsterdam, taking a more southerly course than usual made an unexpected landfall on the west coast of the continent. They took a very dim view of the place and it was another seven years before anything positive was done about it, the interval being busy, one may assume, with the constantly growing trade and counting the profits of it. Then in 1622 Jan Coen, at that time Governor of the Dutch East Indies, decided he was destined to be the one who finally discovered the Great South Land. In 1623 he sent out two ships. They were to find the coast first discovered by Janszoon in 1606 and sailing along it

> ... push their discoveries even as far south as latitude 50; then to return northwards and finally east, i.e. towards the great gulf, exploring as far as their provisions and water would allow. The two captains had to record carefully everything of importance – the character of the peoples, their mode of government, their religion but especially their trade, industry and wealth. . . . Clearly Coen expected to add to the Netherlands the trading resources of the Great South Land which he still believed to be civilised and wealthy. [Rose, p 137]

For all the high hopes with which it started, the expedition, under Jan Carstenz and Willem van Colster, achieved nothing and the next significant date is 1642, the name Abel Janssen Tasman.

Tasman was a *tarpaulin* as distinct from a *gentleman or merchant venturer*, and thus stands out in the record as a kind of throw-back. Nobody knows for sure when he was born or for that matter when he died but his early life was spent as 'a common sailor', shipping out of Amsterdam. When he was thirty he joined the service of the Dutch East India Company and going out to Batavia, lifted himself by his boot-laces into the command of a coaster. Rose says he had 'a reputation for seamanship but also for close-fistedness with his crew and harshness towards the natives' (p 138).

In 1642 the governor-general, Anthony van Diemen, dispatched Tasman on the voyage with which 'the period of Dutch exploration in the Pacific culminated and ended' (Williamson, p 32). He had with him as chief pilot Frans Visscher and his commission was both brief and specific. He was

> ... to traverse the southern Indian Ocean in latitudes higher than 40 degrees S., the usual southern limit of the Indiamen sailing from the Cape to Western Australia; to pass south of Australia itself and to determine whether or not it was connected with the main mass of *Terra Australis Incognita*; if it was not so connected, to see whether there was open water for a passage across the Pacific to Chile in the belt of westerly winds which lay south of the tropical east-wind belt. [Williamson, p 32]

There are interesting implications in Tasman's sailing orders. First of all one is struck by the breadth of vision shown by van Diemen in ordering such a vast sweep of the South Pacific; then there is the true seafarer's interest in establishing world wind patterns to allow of pre-determined passages; and finally an oblique reminder that the Dutch were still fighting Spain for their independence and would be glad of a quick way by southern latitudes whereby they could mount treasure-raids on Chile and Peru.

Tasman left Batavia with two ships, the *Heemskerk* and the *Zeehaen*, and coming

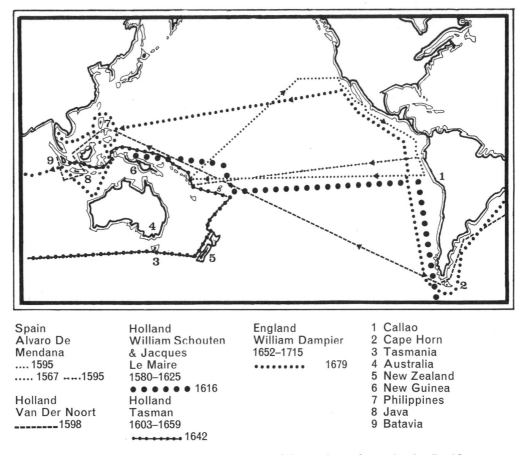

Spain	Holland	England	1 Callao
Alvaro De	William Schouten	William Dampier	2 Cape Horn
Mendana	& Jacques	1652–1715	3 Tasmania
.... 1595	Le Maire	●●●●●●●● 1679	4 Australia
..... 1567 –...1595	1580–1625		5 New Zealand
	●●●●●● 1616		6 New Guinea
Holland	Holland		7 Philippines
Van Der Noort	Tasman		8 Java
———1598	1603–1659		9 Batavia
	●—●—●——● 1642		

48   Routes of the early seafarers in the Pacific

out of the Straits of Sunda, headed for Mauritius, to refresh the crews and check up the gear before taking off into the blue. From Mauritius he got down to what later became known as the *roaring forties*, i.e. the area between 40 and 50 degrees south where the winds are both westerly and wild. Running before them to the east, he made his first landfall not on the continent of Australia, nor on the mythical Great South Land, but on the island now known after him as Tasmania. In accordance with his brief, he left the detailed surveying of his discovery to whoever might follow after, and rounding the island, 'sailed on into the open Pacific'. In doing so he proved that the Dutch discoveries south of Java were not part of a great southern continent reaching to the South Pole and that there could be a southern route from the Spice Islands to America: i.e. one utilising the westerlies of the roaring forties.

His next landfall was 1,200 miles away and came on a coast running north and south. Taking this to be the Great South Land, he followed it northward to a headland which he named Cape Maria van Diemen. This he took to be the most northerly point of the fabled continent, the coast of which he reckoned must run away south-eastwards from there to the region of the Horn.

So with his task completed, Tasman headed for home by the north coast of New Guinea to Batavia. He was utterly mistaken in his interpretation of what was in truth the coast of the North Island of New Zealand, but he had done a very great deal of preparatory work on which others following after him were to build. He made one more deliberate voyage of discovery in 1644, attempting to prove the connection between the coastline of northern Australia and New Guinea; but he missed the Torres Strait and so far as the Dutch were concerned New Guinea and Australia remained 'one continuous land'. The far-sighted van Diemen died the next year and with him went the craving for expansion among the tycoons of the Dutch East India Company. No more is heard of Abel Janssen Tasman and it can only be assumed he went back to hazing crews in the Java coastal trade.

5 WILLIAM DAMPIER (1651–1715)

After Tasman's voyages there was a pause in the process of opening up the Pacific and Heawood has it that 'the hundred years from 1650 to 1750, formed on the whole a period of relative barrenness as regards important discoveries' (p 179). Williamson says of the same period:

> The Dutch, having achieved the monopoly of the Asiatic archipelago and its spice trade, relapsed into the somewhat demoralizing occupation of squeezing the utmost wealth out of the possession, and decided . . . that far-flung new enterprise was neither necessary nor desirable. [p 35]

He goes on to describe the known Pacific Ocean shrinking to a mere pair of thinly used traffic lanes – outward and homeward between Mexico and the Philippines. South of the Line the white man was forgotten and his ships became part of Polynesian folklore. Apart from the steadily increasing numbers of ships on recognised routes the only outstanding voyages in the period were those made by pirates, privateers and buccaneers. Of the last, the best known was William Dampier, another *tarpaulin* if ever there was one, with a history almost too wild, too dramatic and too full of positive achievement for credence.

A brief summary of Dampier's career reads like the outline of an adventure story for boys. At various times he buccaneered in Central and South America, was marooned on the Nicobar Islands, explored in Australia and New Guinea, was wrecked on Ascension Island, went privateering (a polite word for pirating), and rescued Alexander Selkirk (the original of Robinson Crusoe) from the Pacific Island of Juan Fernandez.

49 William Dampier. Drawing by Sherwin after Murray

The exact date of his birth is unknown but he was baptised at East Coker in Somerset on 8 June 1652. His father was a small tenant farmer who died when the boy was seven. The mother quickly followed and at fourteen William was an orphan dependent on the generosity of the squire for his education and God knows what else.

At the age of eighteen, William was apprenticed to a Weymouth ship-master with whom he sailed to the Newfoundland fisheries, where the cold penetrated so deeply into his bones that once he was out of his time he confined his voyaging to the tropics, sailing first to Java before the mast in an East Indiaman and arriving home just in time to enlist aboard the *Royal Prince* for the Third Dutch War. After seeing some service and 'languishing a great while' in hospital at Harwich, he worked his way out to Jamaica with the idea of getting a responsible post in a sugar plantation. But he was soon back in ships and is next heard of with the logwood-cutters in the Bay of Campeachy near Honduras.

Like so many seafarers, Dampier had in him a streak of perversity; he was a congenital non-conformer and the one thing above all else that he refused to stand for was being pushed around. To a large extent he rejected the values of the day; money was nothing to him and the natural wonders of the world his abiding passion. All he wanted was to be able to observe and record, and he trained himself to do this in a scientific way and with such insight and intelligence that his writings, best-sellers 250 years ago, are still vivid and largely as valid as they were when he first published them. He kept a journal which was illustrated with drawings of birds, beasts and flowers, and carried it around with him in a hollow bamboo sealed with wax. Through all his adventures, both disastrous and triumphant, this manuscript stayed with him. Among his writings to survive are:

A New Voyage Round the World, published in 1697 and regarded
    as his most important work
Discourse on Winds, published in 1699
Voyages and Descriptions, published in 1699
Voyage to New Holland, 1703, published in 1709.

He described his *Discourse on Winds* as 'a rude and imperfect beginning of what may better be done by abler hands hereafter' (quoted by Rose, p 161), but it is 'even now deserving of close study,' according to a modern critic also quoted by Rose.

After the publication of his first book, he was lionised by literary society and looked on with great favour by those in high places concerned with overseas trade and shipping. He had a fortune in his grasp then; all he had to do was reach out and take it and the sky would have been the limit. But he wasn't interested; all he wanted was to be out and away again, and the upshot was that the Admiralty gave him command of the first exploring expedition they ever organised.

Dampier's idea was to sail by the Horn and push straight on westwards across the South Pacific till he raised the eastern shore of Australia which was still unknown but already proved to exist by Tasman's circular voyage. In the event, however, the project got tangled up in red-tape and by the time they were ready to sail it was too late in the year to risk the passage round the Horn. Instead, leaving in January 1699, Dampier went via the Cape of Good Hope, western Australia, Timor and the western end of New Guinea, and long before he got that far, he knew he had been swindled. As Williamson puts it:

The organisation and equipment were bad. . . . The ship (the *Roebuck*) was in the last stage of decay, and her rottenness was a crippling handicap to the enterprise. The crew were pressed men, lacking spirit for the adventure and most of them neither physically fit nor experienced seamen. The officers were more inclined to play their captain false than to support him and the first lieutenant professed open enmity and did his best to instigate a mutiny. [p 40]

Sailing along the north coast of New Guinea, Dampier came to the eastern end of it and there to the southward were the hundreds of miles of Australian coastline he had come to discover; and at that point he stopped and turned back, heading for home. This was probably the most perverse thing he ever did and subsequent events proved he was right to do it. One can imagine the decision he faced that day and in the end only applaud the vision and humanity he displayed in taking it, to say nothing of the moral courage. On the one hand the complete fulfilment of the purpose of the expedition lay in his grasp with all the consequent fame and wealth; on the other he was stuck with an ineffectual crew and disloyal officers in a ship so rotten the bottom was likely to drop out of her any minute. If this happened in the unknown, untraversed waters to the south, it would be the end of them all and their only hope was to work her back towards England sticking as far as possible to the recognised shipping routes where they might stand a chance of being picked up when she went. He got her as far as the Island of Ascension in the Atlantic and there on 24 February 1701 she foundered at anchor, but not before the crew had landed safely.

The island was right bang on the main shipping route between European ports and the East, but even so it was several weeks before their distress signals were seen and they were taken off. Dampier himself got home in an East Indiaman, the *Canterbury*, arriving in the Thames in August 1701.

And now he was really in trouble, not for abandoning the enterprise or losing his ship but because somewhere during the voyage he had hauled off and clouted his first lieutenant, a man named George Fisher who had the kind of pull with the Admiralty that Dampier lacked and had always scorned to cultivate. Dampier was brought before a court-martial at Spithead in June 1702. His only defence was a simple, straightforward plea of extreme provocation; but Lieutenant Fisher had spent two years preparing his case. He carried the day and

Having been found guilty of 'very hard and cruel usages towards Lt. Fisher,' for which it did not appear to the Court that he had any grounds, he was fined all his pay for the past three years. . . . 'And it is the further opinion of the Court that the said Capt. Dampier is not a fit person to be employed as commander of any of Her Majesty's ships.' [Lloyd, p 96]

And that was more or less the end of the road for William Dampier. He made two more voyages, one a privateering venture in which he had the command and in which he appears to have reverted to the buccaneer he had been; and the second, another piratical venture in which he was shipped as 'pilot for the South Seas'.

He died, still poor, in 1715 and his name lives on in the Dampier Strait at the north-western end of New Guinea which is the safest passage between the Indian and Pacific Oceans, in Dampier Land north of the pearl-fishing centre of Broome in western Australia and in the Dampier Archipelago off the West Australian coast.

50 James Cook. A
portrait in oils by
N. Dance

6 CAPTAIN JAMES COOK (1728–79)

With the passing of William Dampier the seafarer in general had almost played out his
role as discoverer in the Pacific Ocean. There was still plenty of discovering to be done
but, as in the case of the North-west Passage it was becoming increasingly a task for
specialist explorers rather than a side-line for seamen practising their art in the ports of
the world and on the trade routes between them; the responsibility of governments and
learned bodies rather than the interest and breath-taking gamble of merchant venturers,
shipowners and traders. Nevertheless, one more character – maybe the greatest of them
all – waits in the wings and must be allowed his strut across the stage, for though James
Cook belongs with the specialists, he was first of all and above all else a seafaring man.

He was born at Marton in Yorkshire, the son of an agricultural labourer, and went
to work at the age of twelve for a haberdasher in the village of Staithes near Whitby.
(Williamson has it that the shop was a grocer's and his age was seventeen.) In 1746 he
was apprenticed to a firm of Whitby shipowners engaged in the coal trade between
north-east coast ports and London as well as the Continent.

Cook was another story-book hero and unlike Dampier he had the physique, the
good-looks and the presence for the part. Over six feet tall and built in proportion, he
carried himself like a prince and if ever there was a man born to lead, it was him. The
magnetism, the power of him still comes out of his portrait right across a couple of
centuries of time.

Apart from the rudiments of reading and arithmetic he was self-taught, getting an
incomparable training in pilotage and the working of a sailing ship among the shoals
and sandbanks of the North Sea coast and studying mathematics and navigation in his

51 The *Endeavour* refitting in Endeavour River, June 1770. From
Voyages by John Hawkesworth (1773). Note foretopmast and
spars, anchors, cables and stores landed to lighten ship which
is hove down to get at her bottom

spare time. When his time was served, he sailed before the mast in ships belonging to
other owners and then in 1752 went back to the original Whitby firm as mate of a new
ship they had just acquired. He sailed in her for three years and then, at the age of
twenty-seven, refused command of her, left the firm and joined the Royal Navy as an
Able-Seaman. That was on 17 June 1755. A month later he was made master's mate
and after another six months he was promoted to boatswain. He would have been given
a commission almost immediately, for the special qualities of the man were obvious,
but there had been a scandal about nepotism and such-like in the Navy and the
Admiralty had made it a rule that nobody should be granted a commission till he had a
minimum of six years service behind him. Instead, in 1757 Cook was made *master* of
the *Solebay*, the master being a warrant officer responsible for navigation, pilotage and
the working of the crew. With this rating, Cook played a notable part in the Battle of
Quebec, and his next job, still without a commission, was the surveying and charting
of the coasts of Newfoundland.

This kept him busy until 1768 when at last he was commissioned as a lieutenant
and given command of an expedition to the Pacific. The publicised destination was
Tahiti for the purpose of observing a transit of the planet Venus across the face of the
sun, an event sufficiently rare to be of enormous importance to astronomers; the secret
purpose was to prove once and for all whether or not there was a Great South Land.
Significantly the vessel selected for the task was a Whitby collier originally named the
Earl of Pembroke and now changed to the *Endeavour*. She became one of the most famous
ships ever to sail the seven seas, and more is known about her than of the *Santa Maria*,

the *Victoria*, the *Mayflower* or any other discoverer's vessel before her time. Cook himself wrote of her:

> A ship of this kind must not be of a great draught of water, yet of a sufficient burden and capacity to carry a proper quantity of provisions and necessaries for her complement of men, and for the term requisite to perform the voyage. She must also be of a construction that will bear to take the ground and of a size which, in case of necessity, may be safely and conveniently laid on shore to repair any accidental damage or defect. These properties are not to be found in ships of war of forty guns, nor in frigates, nor in East India Company's ships, nor in large three-decked West India ships, nor indeed in any other but North-country ships such as are built for the coal trade, which are peculiarly adapted for this purpose.   [quoted Williamson, p 95]

The *Endeavour* was built at Whitby in 1764. She was full-bodied, bluff-bowed and slow, but she had a great carrying capacity on a relatively shallow draught and was constructed with enormous strength. Her hull was now sheathed to protect it from the teredo worm. She was of 368 tons burden and had three masts. Unlike Dampier's *Roebuck* of seventy years before, no expense was spared in fitting out and storing her and Williamson says the work done on her after her selection cost almost as much as the original purchase. She was stored for eighteen months and it was Cook himself who decided the scale and nature of the provisions. He also shipped quantities of clothing for the crew, and kept the company small enough to ensure adequate living space for all hands. According to Williamson there were aboard seventy-one seamen, officers and men, twelve marines and eleven landsmen, among whom were included Charles Green, assistant to the Astronomer Royal, and Joseph Banks, F.R.S., a well-known botanist. Banks was a man of wealth and great influence and was able to get the Admiralty to sanction the inclusion of two personal assistants – Doctor Solander, another botanist, and Alexander Buchan, an artist.

Thus there was available roughly an average of four tons of capacity to each man, which was twice as much space as the voyagers of the 16th century enjoyed.

These details are important because they were all part of Cook's carefully worked out plan to defeat scurvy. He knew from his own observation that scurvy and other diseases arose not only because of lack of fresh meat, fruit and vegetables in the diet but also from overcrowded, damp and ill-ventilated living quarters, slackness in personal hygiene, and sleeping in wet clothes:

> He therefore, as a matter of routine discipline, required all quarters to be regularly cleaned and ventilated whenever the weather permitted, and scrubbed with vinegar and fumigated at frequent intervals; and he insisted that his men should at all times be personally clean and well clothed. . . .   [Williamson, p 106]

He also avoided overworking his crew, an exhausted body being a fertile breeding-place for disease. Instead of the usual watch and watch (that is four hours on and four hours off) he divided his foremast hands into three watches doing four on and eight off.

The *Endeavour* sailed from Plymouth on 25 August 1768 and 163 days later his surgeon was able to write in his Journal: 'We passed Cape Horn, all our men as free from scurvy as on leaving Plymouth'; and J. Holland Rose comments:

> Thus at last, after 3000 years of seafaring and generally ill-prepared exploring, an expedition had set forth under the most favourable auspices; for it was headed by an

able and thoroughly trained seaman and hydrographer, with a first-class ship and crew and it proceeded on a well-thought-out quest. . . . [p 194]

In contrast Anson, at an equivalent stage of his voyage round the world less than thirty years before, had lost over 280 out of his 500 men and reached Juan Fernandez with only ten men in a watch fit for duty.

Running on beyond the Horn as far as 60 degrees south, Cook then sailed northwest until he was in the latitude of Tahiti, and running down the parallel he raised the island on 10 April 1769. He was then 260 days out from Plymouth, which was a quick passage for the time. He arrived with the sick-bay unoccupied and had lost only five men on the way; two by accidents on board, two frozen to death on Tierra del Fuego and one who committed suicide. In Tahiti he also lost the artist who died in an epileptic fit.

Cook stayed ninety-three days at Tahiti and his main problem seems to have been the thieving habits of the islanders. Stealing with them was a game developed into a fine art and, as with Magellan in the Ladrones, anything movable was liable to disappear. Cook even had his stockings stolen from under his pillow while he slept and a box of scientific instruments was carted off under the very noses of the sentries. In spite of this quite serious handicap, however, this part of the voyage was a huge success. It 'yielded more definite results for astronomy, ethnology, botany and geology than any voyage yet recorded . . .' (Rose, p 195).

It was the middle of July when the *Endeavour* pulled out from Tahiti and after discovering and spending a month charting the four islands of the Society Group, he stood away to the south in search of the Great South Land. By the beginning of

52   Captain Cook's three voyages

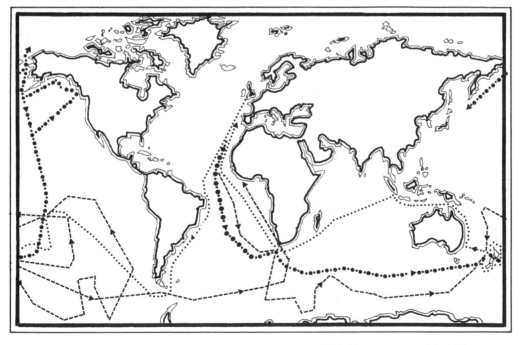

	1768–69 ··········	First Voyage
England	1772–74 ▪▪▪▪▪▪▪▪▪▪	Second Voyage
James Cook		
1728–79	1776 ●·●·●·●·●·●	Third Voyage

53 Death of Captain Cook. By John Cleveley

September he was still sailing an empty ocean and on the 2nd of that month when he was in latitude 40 degrees south, fearful of what the incessant storms might do to his ship and the increasing cold to his men, he put about and, running northwards through 5 degrees of latitude, then headed west for Tasman's New Zealand. He raised the North Island on 7 October 1769 and named his landfall Poverty Bay. Six months later he had circumnavigated and charted the whole of New Zealand and he is commemorated by Cook Strait, the narrows which divide the two main islands and which Tasman had taken for a mere bay.

After another carefully calculated and well-organised stopover in Queen Charlotte Sound to refit and re-provision his ship and rest his crew, he pushed on westward and after nineteen days on 19 April 1770 raised the land again in latitude 37·58 S., south and west of Cape Howe. Heading north, he discovered Botany Bay on 29 April and '. . . surveyed it so well that his chart bears comparison with all the surveys carried out up to 1890' (Rose, p 201).

Still driving northwards up the coast he eventually ran in between the mainland and the Great Barrier Reef, of which he was completely unaware. He was bent on proving or disproving the existence of the Torres Strait and although the going became increasingly difficult because of the mazy shallows and abrupt coral outcrops, he stood on taking every possible precaution. And then quite suddenly his luck, if it can be called that, ran out; the *Endeavour* after sailing more than half-way round the world without a single moment of real drama or grave peril, went up on a ledge of coral and stuck fast.

With any other man and any other ship that could have been the end; but not with Cook and a Whitby-built north-east coast collier such as the *Endeavour*. Never for a single moment did he even loosen his grip on the situation. He lightened her of everything that could be moved including guns, fresh water and most of her spars and she floated off at high water. But she was badly holed and it took a lot of sailorman's know-how to keep her afloat long enough to run into the Endeavour river, site of present-day Cooktown.

It took six weeks to repair her and even then Cook was far from satisfied with her degree of seaworthiness, and headed for the nearest dockyard, which was at Batavia in the Dutch East Indies. On the way he reached Cape York and landing there on 21 August 1770 claimed for England the 2,000 miles of coastline he had discovered. After that he passed through and proved the existence of the Torres Strait, and made Batavia safely in spite of the bad shape his ship was in.

The *Endeavour* was three long months in Batavia and there the sickness and disease Cook had successfully countered for so long, struck his crew – not scurvy but the then endemic diseases of the Indies, malaria and dysentery. Batavia, according to Williamson, was 'the land that kills', and Cook had no defence for his men. Altogether he lost thirty of his company and these, with the eight lost by accident, reduced the survivors to fifty-six out of the original ninety-four. The ship was a slow goer and took three months for the passage home from the Cape, anchoring in the Downs on 12 July 1771.

Cook sailed from Plymouth on his second voyage on 13 July 1772 in another modified Whitby collier, the *Resolution*. His instructions, according to Williamson, were in the main drafted by himself and are succinctly summarised as follows:

> He was to sail to the Cape of Good Hope and thence southwards to rediscover Bouvet's Cape Circumcision in about 54 degrees S. If he could not find this land, or if, after finding it, the sea still appeared open, he was to go as far south as possible and then turn eastwards, circumnavigating the globe in the highest possible southern latitude. . . . By this procedure Cook was certain to encounter any continental land-mass that might exist as far southwards as a ship could sail. It is to be noticed that the area to be covered was not solely that of the South Pacific, but of the Southern Ocean all round the globe. The intention was positively to find *Terra Australis Incognita* or to sail the seas that covered it.
>
> [p 158]

In the middle of January 1773 the *Resolution* crossed the Antarctic Circle, then sailed eastwards through 145 degrees of longitude, zigzagging to and fro in an average latitude of 60 degrees south. Altogether he was 117 days out of sight of land and most of the time encountered gales, heavy seas, fog and ice, both bergs and in the pack.

Heading north in the longitude of New Zealand, he put in at Queen Charlotte Sound to refresh his crew, then sailed south again, this time reaching latitude 71·10 before 'worn to the bone by privations and severe cold' he altered course to the northward again, this time raising Easter Island. Once more he sailed back to Queen Charlotte Sound to recuperate and a third time drove south in search of the mythical land-mass, passing far to the south of and beyond Cape Horn. On his way back he surveyed the south-west coast of Tierra del Fuego, rediscovered South Georgia and discovered the Sandwich Group in about latitude 59 degrees south, longitude 28 degrees west.

He then expressed the belief that there must be a large tract of land near the South Pole, owing to the many islands, the excessive cold and the vast floats of ice encountered in the far South – a surmise equally shrewd and correct. [Rose, p 208]

He called it all a 'poor apology for a continent' and turned homeward, arriving in England after an absence of more than three years without losing a topmast.

His third voyage – 1776 to 1779 – had a completely different objective. His brief this time was to 'search (for) a North-east or North-west Passage from the Pacific Ocean into the Atlantic Ocean or the North Sea . . .' (Rose, p 211). The quest was the death of him as it had been and was still to be of so many other great-hearted men. But first he discovered the Sandwich Islands better known as Hawaii, struck across from them to the Pacific coast of North America and following it up into the Bering Straits reached a point in $70\frac{1}{2}$ degrees north latitude which he called Icy Cape. There he was halted by an impenetrable wall of ice. He returned to Hawaii to refit and recuperate for another attempt and was tragically, stupidly, slain in an effort to recover a small boat stolen by the islanders.

. . . Cook in his first voyage not only discovered but accurately charted more than 4000 miles of habitable coastline; in his second he dispelled the dangerous legend of the Great South Land and revealed the true South, along with many new islands; and in his third he cleared up the mysteries of the Central and North-east Pacific, besides opening up the northwest American shore to trade and future colonisation. In the handling of both ship and crew during three long and trying voyages, he stands forth a great captain; while his speedy and successful grappling with the dreadful crisis on the Barrier Reef bespeaks the consummate seaman. . . . Finally, no conqueror won for mankind by long and bloody wars a tithe of the new homelands which James Cook opened up by peaceful means. [Rose, p 218]

55 Hadley's Octant.
By George Adams,
1753

And after all that has been said, there still remains his great contribution to the well-being of seafaring men. By laying down and fighting for minimum standards of accommodation and hygiene aboard ship, by insisting on and proving the need for a properly balanced scale of provisions, he showed how to counter the threat of scurvy and reduced immeasurably the hazards of long passages.

In the end, however, the greatest contribution made in this period of discovery to seafaring as a way of life, came from a man who had no claim to the label of seaman at all. He was another Yorkshireman, son of a carpenter, John Harrison by name. Harrison was a clock-maker and quite early in the 18th century he was making pendulum clocks so perfect that they neither gained nor lost so much as a second in a whole month. In 1729 he began work on a marine timepiece or chronometer and six years later produced his No. 1 which when tested on a voyage to Lisbon and back in 1736 proved accurate enough to enable the Captain to correct an error of $1\frac{1}{2}$ degrees in his dead-reckoning on approaching the Channel. This still was nowhere near good enough for Harrison nor was his No. 2 completed in 1739 or his No. 3 finished in 1741; but in 1761 he completed a 'watch-type' timepiece and this, known as Harrison's No. 4, was tested on a voyage to Jamaica from Portsmouth. Three weeks out approaching Madeira the chronometer, compared with dead-reckoning, already showed a difference of just under $1\frac{1}{2}$ degrees, but the landfall proved it correct and at the end of a stormy voyage lasting 147 days the error on it was only 1 minute $54\frac{1}{2}$ seconds – less than 2 miles. In 1764 it was tested again on a voyage to Barbados and back and this time lost only 15 seconds in 156 days.

That was it. With the publication of the *Nautical Almanac* in 1767, the invention of the sextant by Hadley and Harrison's chronometer, the problem of longitude was solved and

> . . . what may be termed the pre-scientific age of navigation was brought to a close. Landmark or no landmark, the sailor knew precisely where he was – or had the means to know. He did indeed at long last possess the Haven-finding Art.   [Taylor, p 263]

And thus the second phase of the history of seafaring might be said to have ended and the third, when the seaman came into his own as the carrier, to have begun.

56   Kendal's copy of Harrison's No. 4

Bibliography

ANDERSON, Romola and R. C.: *The Sailing Ship*. London and New York, 1926

BEAGLEHOLE, J. C.: *Exploration of the Pacific*. 3rd rev. ed. London and Stanford, Calif., 1966

BEAZLEY, C. R.: *Dawn of modern Geography*. London, 1901

BIGGAR, Dr H. P.: *The Voyages of Jacques Cartier*. Publications of the Public Archives of Canada, No. 11, 1924

CARRINGTON, H.: *The Life of Captain Cook*. London, 1939

CHIDSEY, D. B.: *Life of Sir Humphrey Gilbert*. London, 1932

CROFT, A.: *Polar Exploration*. 2nd ed. London, 1947; New York, 1948

DAMPIER, William: *Voyages* (John Masefield's ed., 1906)

GIBBS, Lewis: *The Silver Circle*. London and New York, 1963

GREELY, A. W.: *The Polar Regions in the 20th Century*. London, 1929

HAKLUYT: *Voyages*. London, Everyman ed. (Dent); New York (Viking), 1965

HEAWOOD, E.: *A History of Geographical Studies in the Seventeenth and Eighteenth Centuries*. Cambridge, 1912; New York, 1965

LLOYD, Christopher: *William Dampier*. London and Hamden, Conn., 1966

MADARIAGA, S. de: *Christopher Columbus*. New York, 1940; 2nd rev. ed. London, 1949

NEWTON, A. P.: *The Great Age of Discovery*. London, 1932

POHL, F. J.: *Amerigo Vespucci: Pilot Major*. New York, 1966

PRESTAGE, Edgar: *The Portuguese Pioneers*. London, 1933; New York, 1967

ROSE, J. Holland: *Man and the Sea*. Cambridge, 1935

SANDERLIN, George: *First Around the World*. New York, 1964; London, 1966

TAYLOR, E. G.: *The Haven Finding Art*. London, 1956; New York, 1957

WILLIAMSON, J. A.: *Cook and the Opening of the Pacific*. London and New York, 1948

WILLIAMSON, J. A.: *Voyages of the Cabots*. London, 1937; Cambridge, Mass., 1962

Acknowledgements

THE AUTHOR AND PUBLISHERS wish to record their grateful thanks to copyright owners for the use of illustrations listed below:

His Grace the Duke of Bedford: 41
Bibliothèque Nationale, Paris: title-page, 2
Frank Debenham, *Discovery and Exploration*: 37
The Italian Institute, London: 25
The Mansell Collection: 3
The Mariners Museum, Newport News Va.: 53
Museo Navale, Genoa – Pegli: 21
The National Library, Madrid: 39
The National Maritime Museum, Greenwich, London: 6, 28, 33, 35, 44, 47, 49, 50, 54, 55, 56
J. C. Phillipot, St-Malo: 34
The Portuguese State Office, London: 5, 11
The Science Museum, London: 7, 29
Soprintendenza alle Gallerie di Venezia: 17
The Trustees of the British Museum: 1, 12, 14, 16, 18, 22, 26, 42

and for quotations:

A. and C. Black Ltd for Edgar Prestage: *The Portuguese Pioneers*
Cambridge University Press for E. Heawood: *A History of Geographical Studies in the Seventeenth and Eighteenth Centuries*
Cambridge University Press, London and Cambridge, Mass. for J. A. Williamson: *Voyages of the Cabots*
Columbia University Press for F. J. Pohl: *Amerigo Vespucci: Pilot Major*
J. M. Dent and Sons Ltd and Hillary House Publishers Ltd for Lewis Gibbs: *The Silver Circle*
Hamish Hamilton Ltd and Harper and Row Inc. for George Sanderlin: *First Around the World*
George Harrap and Co. Ltd and W. W. Norton and Co. Inc. for Romola and R. C. Anderson: *The Sailing Ship*
W. Heffer and Sons Ltd for J. Holland Rose: *Man and the Sea*
Hollis and Carter and Abelard-Schuman Ltd for E. G. R. Taylor: *The Haven Finding Art*
Mrs A. Knight for J. A. Williamson: *Cook and the Opening of the Pacific*
Salvadore de Madariaga, A. P. Watt and Son and Collins-Knowlton-Wing Inc. for Salvadore de Madariaga: *Christopher Columbus*
University of London Press Ltd for A. P. Newton: *The Great Age of Discovery*

Index

Printed in Great Britain by Jarrold & Sons Limited, Norwich